PRINCIPLES OF LAW

THE PHILOSOPHY OF LAW

THE DOCTRINE OF LAW AND STATE
ON THE BASIS OF THE CHRISTIAN WORLD-VIEW

BOOK II

Principles of Law

Friedrich Julius Stahl

TRANSLATED, EDITED,

AND INTRODUCED BY

Ruben Alvarado

WordBridge
PUBLISHING
Aalten•the Netherlands

www.wordbridge.net

Table of Contents

General Preface to
The Doctrine of Law and State on the
Basis of the Christian World-View

Together with the *History of Legal Philosophy*, *The Doctrine of Law and State on the Basis of the Christian World-View* comprises Friedrich Julius Stahl's magnum opus, *The Philosophy of Law*. This multivolume production provides us with the philosophical foundations upon which Stahl's career as a professor of constitutional law, as a parliamentarian, and as a statesman in 19th century Bavaria and Prussia was based.[1] It is also unique: it is the only comprehensive work of legal philosophy produced by a modern, post-French-Revolution conservative, to wit, a follower of the pioneer in this regard, Edmund Burke.

Conservatism has always been in need of such a comprehensive philosophical system. For opposition to the Revolution did not necessarily lead to unity of world-view. Many conservatives were Roman Catholic and hence argued for a return to (idealized) pre-revolutionary conditions in church and state, thus for the primacy of the monarchy and the papacy – these generally bore the name Counter-Revolutionary. Others were Protestant, and thus perceived a need to move beyond pre-revolutionary conditions, albeit in a manner which maintained continuity with the political, legal, and cultural inheritance of Europe. Among the latter group Stahl was pre-eminent; he was the first of the so-called Anti-Revolutionaries, who in the Netherlands even formed a political party under the leadership of Guillaume Groen van Prinsterer and Abraham Kuyper.

---

[1]For more on Stahl's life see the forthcoming biography by the translator.

Stahl was a protege of Friedrich Carl von Savigny, himself the pioneer of the "Burkean" world-view in Germany.
Savigny is best known for his argument against codification
and in favor of legal continuity, including the primacy of customary law, as contained in his *On the Vocation of Our Age for
Legislation and Legal Science* (see p. 3 below). Such arguments
were completely in line with what Edmund Burke had argued
in his *Reflections on the Revolution in France* and elsewhere. Savigny
founded what came to be known as the Historical School of
Jurisprudence, perhaps the most influential school of legal science Germany ever produced.

The problem with this school was that it lacked a solid
grounding in legal philosophy. Writing in 1901, James Viscount
Bryce, the noted legal historian and diplomat of late 19th-early
20th century Britain, claimed that in view of its methodology it
is "more applicable to the law of any particular country than to
the theory of law in general, for the details of legal history vary
so much in different countries that immense knowledge and
unusual architectonic power are needed to combine their general results for the purposes of a comprehensive theory" (*Stud-
ies in History and Jurisprudence*, II, p. 186). Indeed, Bryce considered the task so monumental that he doubted it had ever been
done, though it "may be done, and so will doubtless be done
some day. Everything happens at last."

As a matter of fact, the task had long since been accom-
plished, even by someone "of the requisite capacity" as stipulated by Bryce. In fact, Stahl had already published the first
edition of his *The Doctrine of Law and State on the Basis of the
Christian World-View*, presenting a legal philosophy sprung from
the loins of the Savignian historical method, back in the 1830s
when he was a young law professor in Bavaria. Savigny recognized it as providing the essential underpinnings in eternal veri-

ties that he himself had failed to produce.[2] And in providing this service, Stahl not only gave the Historical School a philosophical basis, he gave the Burkean common law school of thought a basis as well, although the Anglo-Saxon world of jurisprudence was unaware of it, then as now.

The English common law has never enjoyed the philosophical attention that has been lavished on Continental legal systems. The reason is of course its being a product of court practice without being made the continuous subject of scholarly analysis, as was done on the Continent. Even so, this did not preclude the development of a unique legal philosophy which, although it did not attain to the sophistication of Continental efforts, nevertheless developed into a full-fledged philosophical jurisprudence in its own right, inoculating the legal system from the challenge of natural-rights jurisprudence and enlightened-despot codification efforts the likes of which took over on the Continent during the 18th century Enlightenment. The common-law approach pioneered by Edward Coke, John Selden, and Matthew Hale (Coke and Hale were chief justices) provided the basis for Burke's political philosophy. And from this root came the Continental resurgence of conservatism, which had been driven out of business by Enlightenment rationalism.[3]

---

[2]For an alternative interpretation of this development, see John E. Toews, "The Immanent Genesis and Transcendent Goal of Law: Savigny, Stahl, and the Ideology of the Christian German State," *The American Journal of Comparative Law*, 37, no. 2 (Winter, 1989), 139-169; idem, *Becoming Historical: Cultural Reformation and Public Memory in Early Nineteenth-Century Berlin* (New York: Cambridge University Press, 2004), ch. 5: "The Tension Between Immanent and Transcendent Subjectivity in the Historical School of Law: From Savigny to Stahl."

[3]On this most interesting history, see Harold J. Berman, "The Origins of Historical Jurisprudence: Coke, Selden, Hale," *Yale Law Journal* 103, no. 7 (1994).

Regardless of the success this approach had both in preserving English common-law traditions and in reinvigorating Continental common-law traditions, in terms of legal philosophy it remained rudimentary. William Blackstone's *Commentaries on the Laws of England* (1769), which served as target practice for Jeremy Bentham and his utilitarianism, is paradigmatic in this regard. Indeed, from Bentham onward it might be stated that utilitarianism and pragmatism have been the leading philosophical approaches for dealing with the common law (e.g., Oliver Wendell Holmes, Roscoe Pound). And that legacy lives on into the present day (as witness its latest iteration, "Law and Economics," as exemplified in the work of Richard Posner and Richard Epstein). The alternative is a natural-rights school of thought based essentially on John Locke and the *Declaration of Independence*, and which in consequence is constantly fighting a rear-guard action against French Revolutionary principles.

It might seem anachronistic that help on this front would come from, of all places, pre-Bismarckian Germany. But the sense of anachronism fades when one realizes the affinity between the pre-Revolutionary Continental and English legal systems. It is the divergence between these two which is constantly emphasized; but how is it, then, that Burke could postulate a fundamental legal continuity across Western Europe which was only ruptured by the French Revolution? Indeed, Savigny and his followers recognized in English common law a cognate legal system to the German pre-codification legal system. Which is what makes Stahl's legal philosophy so interesting to common-law legal science. Stahl provides principles applicable to the English common law as well as Continental law, for he draws upon the common inheritance of Western legal science such as described in part by Harold Berman in his *Law and Revolution,*[4] a legal science sharing essential characteristics, maintaining similar institutions, pursuing similar goals.

What Stahl does is provide an understanding of the solid, unchanging foundations to the evolving, adapting thing which is the common law. Considerations of utility and pragmatism are made subordinate to principles of justice and what he calls providential purposes, within the context of historical development. Burke's partnership "between those who are living, those who are dead, and those who are to be born"[5] finds a distinct echo here, as does his conceptualization of rights as inheritance rather than *a priori*, a-historical givens. Likewise, rights are made subordinate to law rather than being the source of law as conceived by the natural-rights school. What's more, Stahl provides subjective right with a clear position and demarcation within the legal system, which is a feat in itself and, perhaps more than anything else, is needed in today's confused, rights-bloated jurisprudence.

The concept he uses to establish these foundations is that of a *doctrine* of law and state. In the introduction he provided to Volume II as a whole (see below, p. 1), Stahl explains this notion of doctrine: it is something other than jurisprudence on the one hand and legal philosophy on the other. Jurisprudence is the science of a particular legal system as it exists in a particular country at a particular time; legal philosophy is its opposite, bringing "law and state into connection with the highest cause and the final goal of all existence" (p. 3). The doctrine of law and state occupies an intermediate position. It generalizes from jurisprudence while it particularizes from legal

---

[4] Harold J. Berman, *Law and Revolution: The Formation of the Western Legal Tradition* (Cambridge, MA: Harvard University Press, 1983).

[5] Edmund Burke, *Reflections on the Revolution in France* (Oxford, England: Oxford University Press, 1993), p. 110.

philosophy. It operates in terms of universals but fleshes out those universals in terms of the particulars provided by jurisprudence. In so doing it provides universal criteria out of which particular legal systems can be generated and by which they can be judged.

Stahl bases this doctrine of law and state on the Christian world-view: because historically the nations of Western civilization likewise were based on that world-view, and because every such universal doctrine must base itself on one worldview or another. "Every philosophical system of whatever name in the final analysis rests on a foundational presupposition that is nothing more than faith, no matter what claim it may make to so-called scientific certainty" (p. 3). So, ultimately Stahl provides us with a Christian common-law legal philosophy, in doing so epitomizing the Western legal tradition in its conservative variant.

Preface to the *Principles of Law*

This book is a translation of Book II of *The Doctrine of Law and State*, originally entitled "The Law" [Das Recht]. The title I have given it better reflects its contents: it contains the principles, the nuts and bolts, of Stahl's doctrine of law and state which then find specific application in Books III and IV, on private law and state law, respectively. It is, as it were, the wheelhouse: here in concentrated form are the elements which distinguish Stahl's common-law, Historical School approach, cast in terms of his Christian faith.

The Christian difference to the legal order is not to be found in any religious test or requirement of conformity but in a defense of the Christian character of legal institutions. Stahl accomplishes this by making institutions rather than actions the cornerstone of law. Law is a general rule, not a specific command; and institutions, not persons, are its object. Persons operate within the framework established by law, but that law is an external, objective framework, not an internal, subjective one. The right of the person and the rights of persons are established and defended precisely by this objectively Christian order. Therefore what is Christian about this legal order is precisely the principles, the law-ideas, upon which it is based, not the level of faith of those living within it. Stahl assumes a Christian society but not individual Christians. In this his approach is similar to that of T.S. Eliot.[6]

This Christian orientation also demands a respect for the inheritance of the nation, conservation of its received institutions and laws – in Stahl's words, "piety" (p. 73 below). It calls

---

[6]*The Idea of a Christian Society* (London: Faber and Faber, 1939).

for obedience to the laws even where they might conflict with justice and the law-ideas, precisely because it recognizes the God-sanctioned authority of law and state as established by the people as something inviolable and as something to which God Himself has commanded obedience. Such an approach rules out a Lockean "right of resistance," but so does it rule out a judicial activism which would overthrow laws on the basis of higher principles of justice. Law is rooted in custom and tradition, supplemented through legislation; only then do the courts have a voice, and it is a derivative, not an original one. The courts are bound to the law as the expression of the historical people, not ephemeral public opinion.

Key elements of the principles of law:
- law and state are dimensions of God's world order, but are entrusted to the people
- law therefore is a product of a specific people, of a nation
- law is historically conditioned: it is therefore not a mere product of the legislative power
- law is positive, which means:
  - natural law is not enforceable law
  - the law which is enforceable is that which has been previously established as law
  - enforceable law is established through custom and legislation, not by judges: judges are bound to the positive law and may not legislate from the bench
- principles of justice and ethics find their incorporation in the law through the medium of the people (custom) or the ruling authorities (legislation)
- the right of personality is natural, concrete rights are acquired

A Synopsis of the Principles of Law

Law and Morality

Law is an outward, external order, and it is an order to be established by the human community as its own order. It is an order entrusted to the people, and although the people have this trust in subservience to God, they are independently empowered to generate and enforce it. Morality, by contrast, is an affair of individuals, of inward fulfillment, of positive virtues. Law is the order of the general rule and the common condition, morality is the order of the particular act.

Law concerns institutions. These institutions – personality and property, marriage and the family, local community, station, the state, the church – are the objects which law aims to maintain and promote.

The purpose of law is both to maintain God's order and to establish individual rights: God not only requires obedience, He provides individuals with the room to develop and establish themselves in the world. "These are the two factors of the ethical world: ethical power with its commands, and man in his free personality, which through law receive their determinate, precisely circumscribed validity in common life" (p. 16).

Law is grounded in the purposes established by God in the natural creation. These natural, factual functions (i.e., possession, procreation, community) form the kernels of legal institutions such as property, marriage, and the state. This is Aristotle's principle of entelechy properly understood. Law is thus rooted in material life and must accord with it.

Law does not command specific acts; it is a general rule. It therefore establishes negative boundaries rather than positive performances. "Law is not to realize the ethical idea of every institution in its positive content, but is only to preserve its most outlying boundaries, only enough to preserve the concept, to keep its opposite from manifesting itself." For law to command positive ethical fulfillment would be for it to become totalitarian; it would destroy individual freedom "and with it true ethics" (p. 20).

Justice, for its part, is not the formative principle of law – that principle is the inherent principles of natural life. But justice ensures that the principle of personality is preserved within those legal arrangements. Together with life purposes, justice determines law, ensuring that it responds to personhood.

The relationship of law to the state is twofold: the law requires the state for it to maintain itself in human life, while the state requires the law as the source of its very existence. Together they form the civil order. No "state of nature" preceded the establishment of the state per se – in this sense, the state is natural, not the product of human choice.

The major error of modern legal philosophy is its natural-rights orientation, in which the state and law are made the creatures of individual choice, where individuals through a social contract choose to leave the state of nature and form a government and a set of laws under which to be ruled. Furthermore, the principle upon which social life is supposed to have been established has been steadily watered down from Grotius's "desire for community" to Thomasius's "pursuit of happiness," finally leaving us with Kant's "live and let live" principle of coexistence as the only bond of the social order. This whole approach is oblivious to the fact that human social order is a higher order transcending individual choice: "In truth, the life of human commonality (the people) is not mere coexistence... rather, it is the common unified fulfillment of a higher order, the ethical world plan; the freedom of individual men is not the sphere of law, but only a part of it" (p. 27). Hegelian and other forms of "organic" philosophy, despite their shortcomings, have restored the recognition of this supra-individual concept of legal order.

Positive Law and Natural Law

The two great errors of modern legal philosophy are either to make natural law into a directly applicable legal standard or to abandon law to the play of interests, cutting off any influence from higher principles. Neither is appropriate. There are two principles to be affirmed in this regard: 1) positive law is law in the strict sense: there is no other law, and as such it is owed obedience; 2) positive law is to be subordinated to "law-ideas" (the principles of law as described in Ch. 1), but only during the phase of legal formation by authorized organs, not by individual citizens – the sources of law are to be subordinated to the principles of law. God's divine order is the archetype of law, but it is not directly applicable as law. In fact, God commands that the law as it stands is to be obeyed, regardless of its correspondence to the principles of law. Human freedom under God is the freedom to crystallize and make concrete those principles of law as a positive legal order. Natural law lacks objectivity, universal recognition, publicity in the sense that it can be known by everyone ahead of time; it therefore cannot be enforced by the state. In fact, to do so is to establish opinion and thus injustice as law. "The rule of natural law is therefore in truth only the establishment of the arbitrariness of every opinion regarding the common public order, it is the establishment of the war of all against all" (p. 38). This was the principle underlying the French Revolution.

Besides the principle of subjection to the law-ideas, positive law is generated in terms of historical continuity. Continuity is crucial to the regard for law, for if law is created in a haphazard, arbitrary fashion by lawmakers from above, it loses its sanctity as the expression of the "wisdom of the ages." The primitive condition in which law, justice, morality, and the like exist commingled, without distinction one from the other, is left behind; but in this process of differentiation, if continuity is maintained, then the original correlation of law and justice is never lost sight of.

The law as revealed in the Old and New Testaments serves two purposes: as a source of law-ideas, on a par with reason and conscience; and as the source of specifically revealed law unique to it, such as Sabbath regulation, marriage among close relations, divorce, and church law. Hence, "the commands of the Christian revelation, like those of reason and justice, form a binding standard for the establishment of law, a claim on the legislator. They are this however in far higher degree and in an entirely different form than the latter because they enjoy the special sanction of God, and because He Himself indicated their particular form, which otherwise is left to human freedom" (p. 43). The Christian nations of Europe in particular are bound to this law, Christianity having been formative to their development.

Modern natural law theory has gotten to the point that it accepts natural law as a subsidiary source of law in addition to positive law. Against this, the Historical School of Law made the advance of recognizing in positivity the true nature of law, rejecting the direct enforcement of natural law by the state. It, however, must guard against the opposite error of rejecting subordination to the principles of law altogether.

The Romans were the first to realize the principle of the positivity of law in its purity; it is a misreading of the sources to attribute to them notions of natural law.

The Origin and Sources of Law

In that law arises through the human community, it takes two basic forms, in accordance with the two main forms human community exhibits: statute, via the ruling authorities who represent the people, and custom, or observance by the people themselves.

Custom is the original form of legal generation. It is produced when the people observe certain norms in a certain way over a period of time such that those norms-in-practice come to be considered a part of the social fabric enforceable by the state. Statute or legislation arises on the foundation of custom; it is generated through deliberation on the part of the ruling authorities and is thus the product of reflection rather than spontaneous generation. Even so, it presupposes custom for its very existence, and must never presume to replace custom.

Neither custom nor legislation must answer to the popular viewpoint regarding law at any given time. Both custom and legislation may at a specific point in history diverge from public opinion. Their validity is inherent in themselves; the law has validity above and beyond what public opinion may think of it. The law is conditioned both by its history and by the principles embodied in it; neither can be discarded should the popular viewpoint change. Public opinion must first be applied through the medium of the sources of law (custom and legislation); therefore its application must answer to the received body of law; there can be no question of willy-nilly lawmaking on the basis of swings in the popular conviction. And if one divorces the law from God and His order as its ultimate ground, one delivers it over to the exclusive dominion of this popular conviction, with all the consequences thereof.

Therefore codification is a bad idea, for it wishes to remake the law in a single act of rational creative power, disavowing the wisdom and the lessons embodied in the received legal order. It is legislation gone haywire, have lost all connection with that order.

Legal science, while not a source of law, is a crucial discipline to the development of the legal order, for it helps to discover custom, to interpret existing law, and consequently to discern the underlying principles of the law, making them available for the future generation of law. In so doing, "it ... brings the latent content of the law to full and harmonious development" (p. 64). For example, legal science played a crucial role in the development of Roman law, apart from any form of legislation. It finds direct application in court practice, through "the evenhanded application of a norm," by which "the courts become the actual organ, i.e., means of determination, for legal science, in the way custom is for the popular consciousness and statutes are for the will of the ruling authorities" (p. 66). Court practice thus takes its place alongside custom and legislation as a third source of law, albeit a derivative and not a primary source.

The legal order as so construed is one in which the law places great stock on historical continuity, in fact as inheritance. It was the Historical School of Law, especially Savigny, who brought this truth to light "in the teeth of the leading orientation of the times" (p. 73). The natural-law school of thought had even gone so far as to consider language to be the product of convention, of mutual agreement.

The Popular Character of Law

Although not the expression of public opinion, law is an expression of popular character. This is the consequence of law being the vocation of a people, of a nation. Every people and nation has a specific character. This character as expressed in the law is the popular character of law. Thus peoples and nations are the proper subjects of law. This does not absolve peoples and nations from the obligation to submit to God's order and commandments; rather, it locates the appropriate basis for realizing that order in free expression. The principle of popular character embodies the idea of the nationality of law, that law is in principle indigenous rather than being imposed from the outside, and that of the popularity of the law, meaning that law is to be generally comprehensible and accessible.

Roman law occupies a peculiar position here in that it has had such an impact historically especially on German law. The popular character of the law does not entail the rejection of this influence, not even of the Reception of Roman law in Germany. The Reception is a fact of life that cannot be undone; furthermore, it mainly affected areas of private law in which indigenous German law was undeveloped.

The popular character of the law has been subverted into the principle of popular sovereignty over the law. In this approach, the popular conviction and public opinion are made into direct sources of law, rather than being mediated through custom and legislation. It leads to the condition wherein the law can be changed from day to day, wherein there is no continuity, no predictability, hence no chance to anticipate future conditions. Such a notion of popular character runs directly contrary to that of the Historical School, which views the people in terms of the historical continuum, not the isolated present.

Legal Obligation

Legal obligation is twofold: the requirement of the ruling authorities to uphold the law, and that of the people to obey it. It is a restricted obligation, in that it, in line with the distinction between law and morality, does not require specific performances but rather prohibits infringements of the general rule which is the law.

Rights: Law in the Subjective Sense

Rights form an essential component of the legal order. They are the expression of subjective personality within the objective common order. They are the expression of a person's inherent ethical power vis-a-vis others, leading to duties on the part of others. But rights are not the be all and end all of law; rather, they form a secondary principle of the legal order. The primary principle is the life purposes ingrained in the natural order, which provide the basis for rights and brings them into coherence.

Rights are not derived from duties; much rather, rights create duties. But rights and duties find a higher coherence in the concept of vocation. Vocation determines both rights and duties, and serves as their standard of judgement. "It is the *ethical, specifically Christian conception to consider rights only in the light of vocation*" (p. 100).

Rights are of two forms: innate and acquired. Innate rights are: "life, liberty, honor, afterwards the general capacity for property, family, political and ecclesiastical rights" (p. 103), while acquired rights are all those rights actually formed through that general capacity. Therefore, many so-called natural rights are actually acquired rights and so cannot be considered to be the portion a person has by nature, such that the lack thereof (e.g., property) can be considered a violation of such rights. It was the error of the French Revolution to confuse acquired rights with rights such as they would exist in an ideal situation. But, as Stahl points out, "There exists just as little an opposition and a dividing line between primeval [i.e., natural] right and the rights of positive law as between the law of reason and positive law. In terms of his idea (thus by nature), man of necessity has rights just as the community has a legal order, but which rights he has is everywhere first more specifically determined by positive law" (p. 104). The Revolutionary doctrine is to consider property, participatory government, and the like to be the natural birthright of all people the absence of which indicates an unwarranted deprivation, while in reality these are institutions subject to development through positive law, without a priori specification. They are the product of the advance of civilization, not the properties of an original state of nature.

The System of Law

Legal institutions are the formative components of the legal order. Such institutions are "complexes" of factual relations put into a legal form based on life purposes. These legal institutions stand in reciprocal relation to the factual relations upon which they are based, both influencing them and being influenced by them. The sum total of these legal relations integrated into a coherent whole is the legal system.

Every people forms its own legal system, each however merely adapting those general legal institutions in terms of specific conditions.

Rights are always a subordinate component of the legal system, they are determined by legal institutions and therefore are creatures of those institutions. Therefore law is not primarily freedom and entitlement, but order, and the legal system is not a coherency of rights but of orders (legal institutions).

Private Law and Public Law

The legal system has two main areas, private law and public law, corresponding to the dual relation of common life, which is individuals in themselves and individuals as members of the whole. Private law serves the purposes of the individual, public law those of the whole. Private law involves integrity and freedom of the person, property, family; public law, state and church. The principle behind public law is not common utility but a common rule, thus a higher order above utility.

Civil Justice and Equity

Civil justice is justice as applied in the civil order. It has two main forms, protective and retributive. Protective justice serves to restore infringements of rights, where such infringements do not likewise involve an attack on the legal order itself, or on the authority of the state to maintain that order. It is satisfied when the wrong is righted by way of compensation. Retributive justice, on the other hand, is meted out by the state as a violation of its own right, as it were; the state punishes those deeds done with an eye to the active frustration of the maintenance of legal order. "This is the concept of *crime*, and its consequence in terms of justice is punishment as restoration of the regard for the violated legal order" (p. 126).

For its part, equity stands in opposition to the law, restoring an original equality of advantages and disadvantages where the law does not obtain, as for instance in a situation of confused boundaries. Where entitlement does exist, equity cannot be called upon to overrule that entitlement. The Romans had a system of equity (bonum et aequum) which they set up to make up for shortcomings in positive law (strictum jus). Where equity is applied, it does not express an objective norm nor the national conviction, but rather, since it attaches only to the particular case, it is solely personal judgement without fur-

ther effect. In that sense it is thus a subjective rather than objective principle.

Notes on This Edition

The edition used for this translation is the 3rd edition of the *Philosophy of Law*, published by Mohr of Tübingen in 1854. I have endeavored to adhere as closely to the literal text as possible while maintaining readability. This included maintaining sentences and paragraphs as they stand except where they seemed overly unwieldy. Words in German which are susceptible to multiple meanings or the meaning of which was not totally clear have been left embedded in the text in square brackets. Section headings do not appear in the original: they are of my own device. My annotations are indicated by the initials RCA. These could have been greatly multiplied, but I have refrained from doing so, secure in the conviction that a quick reference to an Internet search engine, Wikipedia, and the like, would serve the purpose just as well, thus greatly reducing the need for such an apparatus.

Introduction
Regarding the Doctrine of
Law and State

§. 1.

The standards of law and the institutions of the state differ across different countries and times and, being the work of man, everywhere and of necessity contain bad as well as good. There is indeed however something higher, something universal, at work in all creations of law and the state, which purposes to be consummated in all of these, the consummation or lack thereof amounting to the superiority or poverty of the same: that inward unchanging essence [Wesen] of law and state. Now jurisprudence is the science of law and state as it exists in a particular time under a particular people. From this stems the requirement for a higher science, having as its object this inner unchanging essence of law and state. It may be called the *doctrine of law and state*.

Its task is firstly that deeper scientific knowledge itself. In consequence, however, it also serves practical ends, the purer application of law, the recognition of existing legal institutions, the standard for their development.

§. 2.

Law and state rest on the one hand on natural laws, the external conditions of human existence; from this perspective the doctrine of law and state is a *natural doctrine of the state*. On the other hand, law and state rest on ethical demands, and from this perspective the doctrine of law and state forms part of ethics, the character of which is completely opposed to the natural sciences. Ethics has to do with laws found only in the will; the given material – law and state in their factual existence as they have developed through human choice – is not, as with the natural sciences, its unconditional standard and archetype; in part it is concerned with material that is not even extant, with law and state as the people ought to shape it, as history will shape it.[7] The source of knowledge of this ethical dimension is however a dual one: actual legal structures and their historical development outside of us, in which that nature of law necessarily must manifest itself, and the ethical standard within us.

§. 3.

The doctrine of law and state is not separate from positive legal science. Much rather, the latter cannot truly scientifically be pursued without becoming the doctrine of law in one degree or another, i.e., without penetrating into the inner universal nature of legal institutions, while the former cannot recognize the inner universal nature of legal institutions apart from determinate positive, albeit varying, legal institutions. To the degree that the doctrine of law and state is obligated to take its cue from positive legal institutions, it may make use of this or that particular example as the basis and goal of its considerations; and it has the authorization and in fact the vocation to select its own times and its own homeland for this purpose.

---

[7]For this reason a natural science of the state is well-founded which restricts itself to illuminate only one aspect of the state and precisely the lesser, and not law and state as a whole (Leo).

§. 4.

The inquiry into the essence of law and state may set itself the goal of a greater or lesser degree of penetration. If it goes as far as to bring law and state into connection with the highest cause and the final goal of all existence, it is *legal philosophy*. The doctrine of law and state is not usually considered to have to venture this deeply; there is thus a doctrine of law and state as a science over and above positive jurisprudence which for all that is free of all philosophical admixture.[8] On the other hand, legal philosophy cannot be of the sort that derives its entire content from those highest relations. There is much too much human freedom and earthly contingency – perhaps, one dare add, divine positivity – keeping us from fathoming the borderlines and connections between reality and eternal principles. The highest that human science may hope to achieve is therefore simply *a doctrine of law and state on the basis of philosophy*.

§. 5.

The conception of things in their all-encompassing interconnection according to their highest cause and their final goal is what we term world-view. Every philosophical system produces such a world-view. Every religion, and certainly the Christian, contains such a world-view, though not always with the same degree of realization. We base the doctrine of law and state upon the Christian religion. Right from the start we are justified in this by the external legitimation that nearly all European states, and especially Germany, have this religion as their

---

[8]Examples include Savigny's *On the Vocation of Our Time for Legislation and Legal Science* as legal science, and Burke's, Genz's, and Dahlmann's political writings as political science.

factual foundation, and that the majority of persons, even those having rejected the Christian confession, still have not broken in any way with the Christian world-view. The inner justification, however, the one that tips the scales of scientific proof, will be provided, we hope, by this presentation. The scientific confirmation of the Christian world-view cannot extend so far, however, as to make faith optional for its acceptance. Science can only make room for faith, not render faith superfluous. Only keep this in mind, that such is no less the case with every other world-view as well, even those schools of current philosophy that oppose Christianity. Every philosophical system of whatever name in the final analysis rests on a foundational presupposition that is nothing more than faith, no matter what claim it may make to so-called scientific certainty. Even unbelief is a faith – one cannot reason from naked doubt. We have no immediate or homogeneous view of the highest principles of things and thus no absolute certainty; therefore for philosophical systems a purely objective knowledge independent of all personal judgment, such as mathematics, the natural sciences, or even the positive sciences, is ruled out (see I. §. 21).

Accordingly I cannot refute the charge that the philosophical foundations contained in the first book of this work[9] will in part remain unacceptable to those who categorically reject the Christian revelation; I may however respond in the same way regarding every other philosophical exposition. With regard to the subsequent exposition of the doctrine of law and state, however, in that it deals with immediately present, observable things, I do make a claim to the objectivity that makes

---

[9]Book I of Vol. II, *The Philosophical Foundations* – RCA.

its results scientifically certain through the internally consistent explanation of the subject matter.

Chapter One
The Concept of Law
and Its Relationship to Morality

§. 1. Law as the Outward Order of Human Community

The place which law assumes within the entirety of the ethical field has already been shown [in Book I – RCA].

The ethical field has two relations: the *image of God* in *persons* and God's *world order* in the *human race.* The former is the likeness to God, holiness, to which each person is called, each for himself. The latter is the form and order that God ordains for the entire human race in its common life, its common uniform existence, the edifice of social relations He established for mankind's natural preservation and ethical fulfillment, the plan of the ethical world. The former is concerned with the *virtues* (truthfulness, courage, love, compassion, continence, ascesis [Unsinnlichkeit]), the latter with *institutions* (protection of life, property, marriage, respect for elders, ruling authority [Obrigkeit]); each in mutual permeation and unity (I. §§. 25, 26, 30).

While the preservation of the image of God in man is God's business, through His commands and His inner power in the conscience and the free fulfillment of men, the human community itself is to uphold God's world order in the human race through a *human order;* an order which it is to establish and under which it is to subordinate all individuals through outward power. This order is *law.*

God Himself does also maintain his world order in the human race, and He does so directly, through His commands and His power in conscience by means of the free fulfillment of individuals. Lacking this, the edifice of the ethical world would collapse, security of life, property, and ordered family could not exist; indeed, these realize their fulfilled existence in accordance with their full requirement purely and simply through conscience in free fulfillment. However, in order for God's world order not to be dependent on the conscience of individual persons but to exist regardless, uninterruptedly, at least at a bare minimum, at the furthest limit of His commands: for this reason human community shall establish the order of law over all individuals.

There is a dual ground for this: firstly, given the fortuitousness [Zufälligkeit] of human fulfillment – in fact, the dominant tendency to disobey God's commands – God's world order would not be maintained without such an order of law, and while there would be individuals acting ethically, the collective existence of the human race would not exhibit an ethical form and could not maintain itself against the destructive power of evildoers. Secondly, the maintenance of God's world order by the human race is itself a fulfillment of human existence and therefore itself an essential part of this world order. For in this the ethical will of the human community as such, as a unity, reveals itself to fulfill God's commands. Even if men truly out of conscience refrained from murder and theft, lived in monogamy and raised their children, honored their parents – that would only be the ethical deed of individuals, each for himself; God's world order as a whole, however, should also be the ethical act of the human race as a whole.

Now then, in accordance with the self-reliance and unique originality [Ureigenheit] that runs through the entire realm of personal being, the human community is to establish this order, through which it maintains God's world order, *on its own as its own order*. In return it is to give shape to the ideas of the world-plan, which in themselves are a creative conception of God, with creative spirit, each community according to its own understanding and natural disposition in terms of time and lineage [Stamm] and in accordance with its wisdom regarding the prevailing situation; it shall even combine and permeate these with its own humanly proposed [vorgesetzten] goals and establish and maintain the thus-formed order under God's authorization [Ermächtigung] by virtue of its own regard [Ansehens]. That is the high position and worth to which the human race is called, that it not simply fulfill God's commands but that it also establish and maintain this order as an instrument and vessel of world rule under God's influence. Man thereby assumes the godlike position of ethical steward, of lawgiver and judge.

For this reason, this order is entrusted to the *people*, whether natural or politically-formed, because only a people has the unity of world-view and the seeds of creative formation – being in fact a form of higher personality – and for this reason such an order is not charged to the people as a mass of individuals but in their unity, that is, in their organization as a state, in their obedience to ruling authority. In fact, the ruling authority is itself the highest element of that order.

This is the sphere of civil order – the sphere of law and state – over against the spheres of religion and morality; an external kingdom, founded on authority and the arrangement of human ruling authority, over against the kingdoms founded on God's immediate command and immediate power in conscience. This is the origin of that *dualism of commands*, moral and legal. For God Himself there is no dualism. His image in man and His world order in the human race are set in complete unity and agreement through His ideas and are effectuated through His command made known in conscience. However, with that world order also being entrusted to human ruling authority, independently, and thus in certain situations outside of God – for this reason a second ethical order arises, law, separated from the original divine order, deviating from it, in fact often opposed to it.

Law therefore is the life-order of the people and of the community of nations for the preservation of God's world order. Although it is a human order, it serves the divine order, is determined by God's commands, is founded on God's authorization.[10]

The relationship of law to morality (including religion) is this: morality contains God's immediate commands, law the commands of human ruling authority. Morality is an obligation on men, each for himself; law is an obligation on the nation in its unity. Morality includes the entire ethical sphere; law excludes sanctification, the virtues of men, and only includes the ethical construction of human common existence, and even this only in accordance with its barest existence [nothdürftigsten Bestande]. Morality inspires the activity of will of individuals, law an objective external order; the former, ethical action, the latter, an ethical form of public condition; the former, the particular act, the latter, the general uniformly observed rule. All of this will be explained in more detail in the following exposition.

---

[10]The conceptual delineation of law in the second edition of this book was yet insufficient in this point, in that it only brought forth one characteristic, common existence in distinction to individual existence, while leaving aside the second distinction, its being ordered through human community itself and thus human ruling authority as distinguished from an immediate divine command. However, it would be just as insufficient if one were only to bring this second characteristic to the fore, that law is the embodiment of the commands of human ruling authority, for then it would not matter if the ruling authority prescribed ascesis and complete holiness in its commands, and additionally all arrangements of common welfare [polizeilich Verfügungen] would fall within the sphere of law.

§. 2. The Subject of Law: the People

The *subject* of law is the people in *its unity*, thus the *state*, not the individual as such. This means that law is the vocation of the people. It is a command, initially extended to the peoples and their ruling authorities, which they are to realize in their common life. It is required of the people and its ruling authority that public security, property, marriage exist in their true shape; the people and its ruling authority are answerable to God when they tolerate robbery, incest, anarchy. It is similar to what the Apostle Paul wrote to the church in Corinth that "your glory is not His" while one in their midst had taken his father's wife.[11] The individual, on the other hand, stands under the commands of the law only in and by means of the people, as a member of the whole, not immediately for himself, as individual; as *civis*, not as *homo;* he only observes it with an eye to and under the assumption that all others will likewise so observe it. For this reason the standards of law are established through peoples and states, not left to the judgment of individuals, and are maintained by peoples and states, not left to the will of individuals. For this reason, however, only what truly is an obligation of the people, only such actions of individuals the allowance of which holds as an act of the people, as an expression of the ethical judgment and will of the people, belong to the sphere of law. Law is the *common ethos*, the *national ethos.*

Law is nevertheless the vocation of the people only in relation to the *enduring shape of life* which is established to preserve God's world order in the human race. Ethical obligations on the people and its ruling authority when they do not con-

---

[11] I Corinthians 5:6, Luther's translation – RCA.

cern this life arrangement, for example to come to the aid of an oppressed people, to reward a deserving man, are therefore only moral obligations on the nation, not elements of law. Law is the *objective ethos,* the *outward shape of life.*

For this reason law everywhere only includes [begreift] the *ethical rule,* not the ethical obligation of the *concrete case,* and its most prominent characteristic is *continuous realization,* that is, unfailing fulfillment by individuals, uninterrupted continuity on the whole. Law is not a bare norm but an *order:* precisely an implemented, continuously observed norm. The necessity of unfailing fulfillment, which accordingly pertains to the essence of law, is expressed as *physical coercion* undertaken against the resistance of individuals. Coercion therefore from ancient times has appeared the primary, that is, the most evident distinction between law and morality. Hence the ethical power of law is not based directly on ethical ideas, as is morality, but in this external, pre-existing order, and the law precedes the acts of individuals and even the acts of the people, as something already implemented, although it in turn is only implemented in and through this action. Law in this manner is on the one hand an obligation on the will – an *ethical command* – and on the other hand *an institution mechanically preserving itself.* This dual nature is the peculiarity of the law.

§. 3. The Object of Law: Institutions

The *object* [Gegenstand] of law is the institutions [Einrichtungen, Institutionen] of God's world order, thus the relations and bonds among men which make up common existence, which comprise the existence of the human race as a whole. These institutions are the following:

1. The *preservation of individual existence:* integrity and freedom of the *person,* protection in the acquisition and use of means of subsistence (*property*).

2. The *expansion of the race:* the organic bond of procreation, which in the ethical sphere becomes a bond of will, thus elevated to enduring individual shared identity – the *family.*

3. *Common existence as race:* the mutual complementarity of the species [Gattung] in its activity – *local community, estate* and *corporation,* and their common higher rule in accordance with ideas and purposes as an ethical intellectual kingdom – the *state* and the *community of states.*

4. The *common bond with God:* the institution [Anstalt] to reconcile mankind with God and to glorify God through mankind – the *church.*

All these relations, even those initially existing only among individuals, such as for example property and marriage, have the character of *impinging upon the whole;* they are the general bearers of human existence. They stand together in a (not merely logical, but real) unity, while they generate and condition each other. Together they are the natural furnishing for the preservation of the human race and the ethical shape of its common life. They are the plan of the ethical world. For this reason their order is the task of the community, and thus the law.

Excluded however from the sphere of law, and belonging to morality alone, is the entire *conduct of individuals* which either merely concerns oneself, such as truthfulness, moderation, frugality, or, although it involves other individuals, its effect ends with those individuals, such as friendship, gratitude, hospitality. For example, if one were to consider marriage only to be a bond among the two spouses, without its connection

with other marriages [den übrigen Ehen] and the remaining
human relations which make it a general necessary institution,
it would be as little a legal relation as friendship is. Likewise
excluded among these relations of common existence are all
those relations which turn on total fulfillment by individuals
and not merely the preservation of relations in general in accordance with their ethical continued existence. In the family,
for example, the never-ending manifold expressions of love
and piety, which must ever be individual, the value of which
lies in inventive feeling ever creating afresh, are simply of a
moral nature. It is not through them that the individual family
takes its place in the enduring edifice of the general condition.
On the other hand, community of rank [die Gemeinschaft des
Standes], the duty to provide sustenance, the bounds of mutual
esteem must exist in every family in the same manner and with
the same effect. This is the necessary foundation of human
common existence, such that the possibility of dissolving into
individuals must destroy the condition of the whole. Therefore, through these unshakable [unverrückbaren] foundations
operating in the whole, the family enters the objective life-order, the law.

This partition runs through all relations. Accordingly,
individual devoutness or orthodoxy does not form part of the
law and its coercion, though the preservation of the church as
a public institution upon its true foundations, with its pure
doctrine,[12] does; not individual chastity in accordance with the
standard of the Sermon on the Mount, but rather the preservation of marriage as a general institution in its purity (legal prohibition on divorce, polygamy, etc.); not individual probity

---

[12] Here lies the fundamental error in the system put forward by
Thomasius, that because devoutness and orthodoxy are not an object of
external power, church government does not have the task of preserving
pure doctrine.

[Redlichkeit] in property transactions [Vermögens-Geschäft-en], but rather the establishment of general property exchange on the basis of fidelity [Treu] and trust (bona fides). This is the boundary of the sphere of law over against the sphere of morality, the compelling ordinances of the government as against free fulfillment of conscience. Self-evidently this borderline is a fluid one.

§. 4. The Twofold Purpose of Law: God's Order, Man's Rights

The *purpose* of law is the preservation of God's world order, albeit in independent and free human implementation. Its first priority is therefore *God's commands;* its other is *rights.* This is because God's world order does not simply intend [bezielt] the ethical well-being of men but also the natural preservation and the guarantee of their personality, their worth, their vocations; it not only obliges men but secures and shields them as well. And in accordance with the nature of personality, ethical commands to the degree that their content consists in the protection and benefit of men likewise become an ethical power over against others, intrinsic to these men and inhering in them – this is the concept of *entitlement* [Berechtigung] or *law in the subjective sense.* The efficacy of law therefore consists in this, that it establish and secure on the one hand a definite range of inviolable validity for *divine commandments* in human common life, on the other a definite sphere of existence and power for men, that is, *rights.* So on the one hand it sanctions the divine command of pure marriage (monogamy, prohibition on divorce and incest), the divine command of submission to authority (from which also conscription, the duty to pay taxes), the divine command of punishment for murder, theft, incest, blasphemy; on the other hand it preserves for men the right of

life, property, privileges of marriage, the authority of parents
and civil government. These are the two factors of the ethical
world: ethical power with its commands, and man in his free
personality, which through law receive their determinate, precisely circumscribed validity [Geltung] in common life.

For this reason the arrangements [Anordnungen] made
by the ruling authority for common life, even for those institutions of the common condition, are an element of law only
when they have as their object either the commandments of
God or the rights of men. If they on the contrary merely contain technical means on behalf of such commandments or human praiseworthy goals and human utility, they fall under the
area of administration [Verwaltung] and the common welfare
[Polizei]. Everything that above was urged as a component of
the legal order – property, government, punishment for murder, incest, blasphemy – is the assertion or more precise
specification of immediate divine commands: thou shalt not
steal, thou shalt not kill, honor thy father and mother (thus all
ruling authorities), thou shalt not commit adultery, thou shalt
not take the name of the Lord thy God in vain. On the other
hand, such things as military, passport, or post regulations,
instructions for the administration of demesnes [Domänen-
verwaltung], or a decree to lock houses at night, to quarantine
contagious disease, all of these are mere technical means to
safeguard the power of ruling authorities, life, and property, or
for human comfort and mores [Sitte], rather than being immediate results of a divine ordinance. While these certainly may
be categorized as law in a broader, merely formal sense, because they are issued by the ruling authorities and therefore are
legally binding, they are not so in the actual and material sense;
although they are the commandments of legal authority, they
are not themselves components of the legal order.[13]

---

[13]When with us public indecency is punished only in terms of social

This is the delimitation of the sphere of law over against the sphere of administration and the common welfare. As with its delimitation over against the moral sphere, this stems from its concept, which is that it is the human order for preserving the divine world order. Accordingly, everything is excluded that is merely the affair of individuals (*morality*); but no less so everything, even that which is common and public, which is merely technical and cultural/educational [Paideutik] rather than a necessary ethical ordinance in itself (*common welfare*).[14]

---

welfare measures [polizeilich], then that is a symptom of a lax condition of public mores, not a basis for erecting a concept of law and its delimitation over against social welfare. In accordance with the true requirement and the nature of the case, such indecency, to the degree that it falls under the purview of the state, is to be treated as a violation of the public ethical family order in the sphere of law, and thus falls under penal law (albeit in the lowest degree, although classified under the law); the sphere of social welfare in this case only pertains to prevention of indecency (e.g., against offensive dress, movement at night, mixed bathing, etc.), thus only such as the violation of which does not in itself constitute an offence against the divine order.

[14]This yields that which Grotius sought, a concept of "natural law" (the sphere of law) delimited both over against morality and against politics. Usually one sets the criterion of law as opposed to social welfare or other activities of the state in the fact that it determines *rights*. But, as is shown elsewhere, the law does not restrict itself to this, and furthermore this would make social welfare appear only as a higher (objective) goal, law on the other hand as an aggregate of (subjective) entitlements. On the contrary, the law makes the opposite impression, that precisely it is the higher sanctified order, prior to all other spheres of the state. Its field is formed by the institutions of God's world plan and unconditional divine commands, albeit in the freest human implementation, over against other objects of common interests and humanly-proposed goals. Rights are only a part of that sanctified order.

§. 5. The Principle of Law: The Purposes Inhering in Life Relations

The *principle* and *standard* of law, that which provides its commandments with their content, are the concepts and commands of God's world order, thus not, as with morality, the idea of fulfilled personality, but rather the idea of complete common existence, the complete edifice [Baues] of social relations; this is indeed the divine plan for the ethical world, the *ideas of Providence* (1. §. 30). On such Providence is based in equal manner both the factual existence of those relations as natural institutions, and their ethical shape as the ethical world, which is in fact law. The activity of law is therefore the *force of formation* [Gestaltung] *and determination;* by it the separated existences of men and institutions, and their fixed boundaries, arise in the ethical sphere, all the while being related to each other as a coherent whole. It is the development of a world with its determinate constructions [Gebilden], similar to the natural creation.[15] A providential idea inheres in every individual life relation (property, marriage, the parental relation, activity of rank [Standesthätigkeit] and the like), which strives to be fulfilled in it, and the fulfillment of which is the task and criterion of the law. As law is an ethical order founded on natural institution, every legal institution has a natural basis: for example, property is based on possession, marriage on procreation, the state on the union of the forces of the people, etc. The providential idea of that legal relation is already present within this factual basis and is active as a disordered inclination which, elevated to permanence and clear shape, controls that factual

---

[15] It is therefore an error to assume that, assuming the perfection of man, love would replace law. Love can only replace coercion, not law; because love is not form-giving [ist nicht gestaltend].

basis through an ethical, or better legal, norm. So for example in possession, the idea of individual gratification through things; in procreation, the idea of the union of the sexes, etc. The idea of each life relation having a self-propelling action beginning in natural inclinations and progressing to ethical order fulfills Aristotle's view, which he characterized as the τὸ οὗ ἕνεκα, or as the τέλος, that is, an *inclination and purpose of nature* characterizing relations themselves and being realized in them. In accordance with the Christian understanding, however, this likewise appears as a *divinely established purpose* for life relations and as a *vocation* for that purpose established for men. *This purpose* (τέλος) *characterizing life relations is the objective and real principle of legal philosophy* as opposed to all merely subjective or merely logical principles. It is the leading principle in the entire exposition which follows.[16]

§. 6. The Boundaries of Law

The law does not have to take up the ethical ideas inhering in life relations *to their full extent*, but only to the degree that they, in accordance with the above (§. 3), form the permanent,

---

[16]This is however an *absolutely positive* principle, because the purpose of each life relation (family, state) must specifically be recognized as given, which can only be found by its own observation of itself [durch Beobachtung seiner selbst] and not through statutes or concepts outside of and prior to it. Contrary to this, Hegel for example does not make the particular inner significance of property, the family, the state to be the foundation of his assessment; on the contrary, this will issue from the concept of will in accordance with the substantial and subjective moment and, even farther back, the law of dialectic. For this reason it can and doubtless will happen to us that we hit the truth in some matters and err in others, in accordance with whether we have rightly discovered the particular purpose of the one institution, and not done so with another. A legal philosophy with the claim, such as is being made up to the present time, that it is either entirely true or entirely false according to whether its principle (supreme axiom or method) is true or false, is totally foreign to our standpoint.

uninterrupted shape of common existence, and are to exist as the work of the community (the nation) in its unity as manifestation of the ethical spirit of the ruling authorities. Their complete and higher fulfillment, by contrast, pertains only to God's immediate commands and immediate operation in the soul, not to the human order, which is only to support that and therefore is much more the work of public mores [Sitte], which in turn themselves have their source in the conscience of individuals rather than in governmental coercion. Certainly in the given condition of human nature – the separation of the common will from the individual will, and the impurity of each – the sphere of the common condition and therefore of law must be restricted to the *negative* (I. §. 45); that is, law is not to realize the ethical idea of every institution *in its positive content*, but is only to preserve its *most outlying boundaries*, only enough to preserve the concept, to keep its opposite from manifesting itself. So for example the legal protection of personality does not contain the positive recognition of individuality but only the negative, that the concept of the person not be abolished, thus that one not be bodily violated by another, be injured by another; the law of marriage does not include the positive union and devotion of spouses, which public ethical opinion demands as generally necessary apart from all particularization, but only sees to it that polygamy, divorce, arbitrary change of marriage, abandonment, not providing for one's wife, not take place, thus only that the concept of marriage exist. Therefore the law of the state does not require the permeation of the general and the individual, like Plato and Schelling (unjustly) require of the state institution, but only obedience, fulfillment of performances [Leistungen], etc.

Law and morality, the two sides of the human collective ethos, accordingly stand together in a bond of unity. The same ethical (providential) ideas provide the content of law and the content of morality, to the degree that morality is concerned with the relations of common existence: for example, faithfulness and fairness in property transactions, chastity, piety, care, obedience in the family, etc. One may express it virtually definitively like this: the law, like morality, rests on the Ten Commandments and solely on them. Therefore all deeper minds sense that a separation of law from morality in terms of content – such as is done in abstract natural law – must of necessity be untrue. Regardless of this, however, the commingling of these two areas is strictly out of the question, because morality realizes these ideas in their full extent and from their positive side while law realizes them only from their negative side, only at their most extreme limits.[17] Both positions, that the law retain ethical content and be determined by ethical ideas, and that it not incorporate any more of these ideas than belong to its sphere, are likewise necessary for its true operation. Complete or at any rate positive incorporation of the contents of ethics into law and its coercion (§. 2) destroys individual freedom and with it true ethics. On the other hand, leaving this entirely up to individual freedom, e.g., the allowance of concubinage and the like, is in itself unethical simply as lack of

---

[17]This is true even in the sphere of property [Sphäre des Vermögens], although that sphere is usually considered to belong simply to rights. Here as well we do not have mere moral demands of neighborly love, beneficence, etc., regarding use, which however belong to an entirely different sphere, but a *moral probity* of a wider extent than the fulfillment of the law and even lawful *bona fides;* e.g., overcharging in the case of a sale is irreproachable before the law but not before morality, and the moral law against which it offends is by no means the law of love but the law of moral probity as distinguished from juridical, precisely positive probity as opposed to negative, in which one does not deceive or cheat. Another example in which the law is fully satisfied but where on the contrary moral probity (to be distinguished from love) feels outright offended is this: a banker detaches an officer to the army, who immediately after the victory informs him thereof, which information the banker uses by immediately embarking on buying on the exchange.

acknowledgment of the ethical common will, and has the consequence of eliminating the solemnity of the ethical command from the objective shape of life and from constant view, as well as from the public mind, and thereby in the end from ethics itself. So for example the true sentiment [Gesinnung] regarding the ethical essence of marriage is not maintained when divorce is arbitrary or is viewed as being a matter of entire indifference in public institutions. When however public life in its constant appearance displays the purity of marriage, the ethical view of individual persons regarding marriage also receives confirmation. The burial of suicides with all otherwise customary ceremonies must end in smothering the notion of the sinfulness of suicide. The public observance of Sunday, that is, the prevention of workaday labor appearing in public, will actively maintain in the general consciousness the necessity of dedicating this day to religious gathering; and the reverse is also true: it must be left up to individuals to decide whether to observe Sunday or not, etc. This is the general guideline for the level of moral and religious requirement. There is however no clear dividing line, the less so because the given makeup of the human condition – the contradiction between the true ethical shape of life and the human will – should never have even existed, but rather a broad amount of leeway for adjustment according to time and condition, and particularly in terms of the capacity to bear on the part of the persons for whom the laws are to be given.

§. 7. The Place of Justice in Law

These things, the purpose inhering in life relations and the ethical characteristics contained in that purpose, differ for each: freedom and the free expansion of personality, the bond of the sexes, sanctity of mores, honor and piety, etc. But one characteristic runs equally through them all – and that is *justice*. Justice, its essence being to maintain intact regard both for the ethical power and its laws and the right of men in equal inviolability, is the inseparable attribute of all ethical order of law, both divine and human. Every individual relation as well as the entirety of the legal order must be determined in accordance with this, so that both the command of God's providential order and the rights of men owed to them as a person and for each and every relation be manifested and attested in indestructible sanctity. The providential ideas on the one hand and justice on the other are together the poles of the ethical world order. The former determine (objectively [sächlich]) the structure of this order, justice however determines (subjectively [persönlich]) the relation of ethical power established and sanctified by that order to men vested with rights derived from it. The former are the organic constructive power of the world order, the latter its self-confirmation and self-empowerment as a kingdom of living wills under a supreme immutable will. Both of these mutually condition and permeate each other.

Justice therefore is not the sole, nor even the original and form-giving, principle of law. Much rather, it already presupposes a content of commandments and rights which through it are to attain the guarantee of inviolability, and this content stems from the purpose inhering in life relations, in accordance with the plan of the ethical world (§. 5).

The original order of legal institutions (property, marriage, paternal power, state, church) therefore in no way rests on the idea of justice, but rather on other ideas peculiar to each institution in its own right. It is only in accordance with these, not justice, that the commandments which hold for property, for marriage, are determined, as are the rights which are to be ascribed to spouses, fathers, heirs, property owners. However, justice is nevertheless a determining factor in all these institutions to the degree that the right of personality which is bestowed on men from the beginning is to be preserved inviolable in all of them and in each according to its peculiar nature.

Furthermore, justice also has a sphere over which it exclusively and originally rules, appropriate for the preservation of the entire legal order which is its essence. The administration of criminal law in its entirety, the inviolability of positive law, the preservation of acquired rights, the general regard for the merit and guilt of men in all civil and criminal, private and public relations, rests on the concept of justice alone.

Justice is not the original and form-giving principle of the legal order; but it is its preserving and confirming principle, its final seal.

§. 8. The State as the Necessary Upholder of Law

The law *realizes* its existence only through the *state*. Just as the law is the human *order* of common life for the sake of the maintenance of God's world order, so is the state the institution of human *rule* of common life in proxy of God and for purposes set by God. The first of these purposes is however precisely that order.[18] Law and state have an all-encompassing purpose, which is to form the human race into an ethical world. They condition each other mutually in this, but without coinciding with each other. The state derives the norm for its order, and in fact derives its entire existence, through the law,[19]

---

[18]Law therefore comprises all the actions of men, including those done for their individual purposes, and gives them a common rule only for the sake of their common relation; the state, on the other hand, to the extent that it is active, unifies everywhere the actions of men only for common purposes. The former is a norm for life relations, the later is itself a life relation and a real power.

[19]The other relations have a factual or ethical existence apart from all rights (property, family) while the state is a legal institution according to its very concept.

while the law gains its realization only through the state. However, the law orders other relations besides the state, while the state pursues other purposes besides the law. Both together form the concept of the *civil order* (status civilis), and exhaust the ethical world in terms of its objective existence.

A so-called *"state of nature"* neither factually preceded the civil order nor is it scientifically to be presupposed, such that one has first to discover it in order to start out from it as terminus a quo. One only arrives at such starting points when one goes awry and obliterates the entire connection with objectivity, putting himself first (rationalistic standpoint). On the other hand, one may posit the civil order as a given situation over against the state of nature as a conceivable situation in order by these contrasts to illuminate it and confirm it.

§. 9. Misrepresentation of Law in Legal Philosophy

Philosophy, both ancient-pagan and modern-rationalistic, does not see in law what it really is, the order of the living personal God, since it everywhere leaves Him out of consideration. It treats the law just as it does morality, as a command of *reason* (laws of thought, human nature striving after harmony). Because God's influence in the earthly condition is not visible, outward observance also perceives the law as a mere self-contained order, the regard for which is by no means conditioned by faith in God. Such mere outward observance likewise considers morality as independent of faith in God, and nature as existing in itself without a Creator and Lord who grounds and maintains it. This viewpoint, restricted to what is observable on the earth, is considered by that philosophy to be the only scientifically secure one. However, the dualism of the ethical field is inexplicable from this standpoint, because it is based precisely upon the dualism of world-ordering authorities, upon the free world plan of God, that in the law the human race itself is called to a godlike world-ordering position. Both spheres furthermore are presented in an inexplicable inadequacy. Morality, the true ethical action of man, appears fully isolated, arbitrary, detached from a grand plan in which it intervenes, and the law, the ethical shape of the common condition, appears in the unsatisfactory manner of mere human order. It does not yield a world order maintained by God himself and fulfilled through the inward ethical action of man. Finally, there are the inexplicable contradictions in which the law empowers what morality prohibits and reason requires obedience even to irrational law.

Philosophy did not in the same manner close itself off to that other truth, that the requirement of common life, the common order of the human race, termed in an inappropriate expression "sociability" [Sozialität] form the ground of the law. This truth is accessible even in abstraction from God. It was recognized by Aristotle, following him the entire Middle Ages,[20] in the same way by Melanchthon,[21] then finally by the founders of the "sociabilistic" systems (Grotius, Pufendorf) discussed below. However, apart from Aristotle the basis was conceived to be the mere empirical datum of the need for society rather than ethical common requirements, and likewise mutual necessity rather than original unity; this tendency was

---

[20]E.g. Thomas Aquinas, *De regim. Princ.* l. VI. c. 3: "Appetitus videlicet humanus, ad communicandum opera sua multitudini, ut molestum sit eidem aliquid virtutis agere absque hominum societate....– Patet igitur hominum sive ex parte corporis, sive partis sensitivae, sive considerata sua rationali natura necesse habere vivere in multitudine. Ex qua parte necessaria est secundum naturam constructio civitatis". – Nearly all writers of the Middle Ages put the Aristotelian πολιτικόν ζῷον ("sociale animal") at the basis of politics.

[21]Melanchthon, *Phil. Moral* (edit. Basil. Tom. IV.) p. 214: "Homo conditus est ad societatem" – where however follows: "doceantur homines et praecipue de deo."

realized fully by Grotius, who conceived of sociability simply as the instinct of the individual. When, however, Thomasius replaced the drive toward sociability with the *drive toward happiness*, by which the individual of necessity becomes isolated, the last remnant of an objective legal principle was eliminated. For this reason, from the outset it was impossible for natural law in its entire development up until Schelling to discover the proper relation between law and morality, in that it derived everything from the nature of the individual, while the law has its derivation only from the equally original existence and task of the community.

So the ultimate consequence was that one came to the sharply expressed heresy restricting the legal sphere to the *external freedom of individual men* and the *coexistence of this freedom* (Kant, Fichte). Accordingly, the prohibition on polygamy and incest, in fact even the duty to provide for and care for children, was excluded from the legal order, and law generally and everywhere lacked higher sanctification because it existed only for the benefit of man and not for the order of God.

In truth, the life of human commonality (the people) is not mere coexistence; it is not a mere existence of men alongside each other, in which they pursue their purposes as individuals, protect themselves from each other, and at most promote each other; rather, it is the common unified fulfillment of a higher order, the ethical world plan; the freedom of individual men is not the sphere of law, but only a part of it.[22]

---

[22]Now that the nullity of this standpoint and doctrine has been irrefutably demonstrated, the attempt is being made, despite this, by those who cannot separate themselves from it, to introduce it in another, less clear and determinate form. Law is certainly not restricted to the mere freedom of men; nevertheless, its distinction with morality, they say, is that it only establishes *rights of men* (claims), and duties merely as the consequence of the claims of others, while on the contrary morality merely burdens with duties and does not confer rights; or, expressed in another form, law contains the rules which stem from justice, i.e., the "suum cuique," while morality con-

The Greeks, on the other hand, even though they apparently were not yet aware of the distinction between law and morality, nevertheless possessed the elements of a more just distinction, in that Plato distinguished between the justice of man and of the state, and Aristotle distinguished between a ἁπλῶς δίκαιον and a πολιτιχον δίκαιον. Now then, when these distinctions were carried through willy nilly, law seemed merely to be an attribute and tool of the state, and thus both concepts coincided falsely with each other (see above, §. 8).

Lately, *speculative philosophy*[23] emphatically has presented the law as an objective ethos, albeit muddled by the pantheistic dislocation of all viewpoints. This holds mainly for the basic principle of its legal teaching, that of the *"general will"* in the sense in which first Schelling[24] and then Hegel in his own way furnished a system of legal philosophy. This concept, distinguished absolutely from the volonté générale of Rousseau and

---

tains the rules stemming from charity. (For example, Wärnkonig's legal philosophy among others; see thereagainst my anti-criticism in the appendix to Vol. I of this work; apart from this, this viewpoint in a less extensive form is extremely widespread as a remainder of the older form of natural law.) However, religion and morality confer rights (claims) just as well as does law, e.g., spouses and fathers have rights derived just as well from the Gospel as from the civil code, and vice versa, the law itself just as well establishes original duties and requirements which are not the consequence of the entitlement of others as does morality, e.g., the prohibition on incest, prohibition of divorce by mutual agreement, likewise the duty of subordination which inheres in state power and which by no means is the mere consequence (effluence) of the entitlement of men, as well as the entire administration of penal law. In the same manner, many commandments and demands follow from justice which nevertheless belong not to the sphere of law but to the sphere of morality, such as the justice of a father with his children, the justice of a critic, and vice versa, the legal order contains demands and commands that are derived not from justice but from purity of mores and piety; and regarding all of these justice itself is not merely the suum cuique (give to every man his right), but at the same time the soundness of an ethical order (§. 7).

[23]Schelling, *Acad. Stud.* Hegel's *Philosophy of Law*, also Schleiermacher's *Ethics;* cf. Book I of this volume, §. 30 (paragraph 4).

[24]See Fichte's and Niethammer's *Philosophical Journal*, vols. 4 and 5.

Sieyès, signifies a power over individual men which is neither the will of the people (be it as collection of individuals or as a unity) nor the will of God but rather the power and necessity of the *impersonal* (logical) *world law* (in this stage of the development of the *concept* of will) which in a pantheistic manner of speaking is ascribed the attribute of will. Apart from the fact that this conception necessarily denies the existence of a personal will over men – thus God – this "general will" entails that, because in truth it cannot will anything, legal content not be derived from its will (the world plan contained in its creative intelligence) but simply from its concepts and abstract aspects (positing a general possibility, a specific content, and the union of both, etc.).

In this manner Hegel comes to his miraculous [wunderlichen] conception that the ethical world can be dissected into three spheres: 1. Private law ("abstract law"), 2. Morality, and 3. Family and public law ("ethics") , and to morality as the connecting link between private and public law, similar to the way one wishes to conceive of the human soul as a connecting link between the members of the human body.[25] The central meaning of this conception is that it is not the eternal content of the will, love, etc. that is to be realized in human community, but the abstraction of a will-function, of aspects of that which is general, etc.; and the ethical world consists in their realization. If we however prescind from this central meaning and consider the matter simply in terms of its results, there is in these three spheres nothing else presented than three basic forms: human *entitlement* ("abstract law," law of the individual will), human *obligation* ("morality"), and *objective organic connections*. Entitlement, or the law of individual will, consists in property and obligation (contract), in mine and thine;

---

[25]Compare my *Philosophy of Law* (2nd ed.), vol. I, p. 428.

duty ("shall"), in the pursuit of the good; the objective organic communities (ethics), in family, corporation and state. Hereby Hegel falsely states these three basic forms as being in a dialectic development, the one following after the other, thus successively and side-by-side, as three different spheres of life, while in reality all three are equally original, mutually permeating the spheres of life. Entitlement does not stop with property and obligation ("abstract law"), it runs through all spheres (e.g. rights of marriage, royal rights); morality is not restricted to the pursuit of the good but likewise permeates all spheres, even those of so-called abstract law; and objective ethical institutions ("ethics") are not simply the family and the state but also property etc.; for though the latter is no organic connection, like them it is a part of the construction of human common existence. Morality therefore also is not a connecting link between property on the one hand and family and the state on the other, but, to the degree that these are legal institutions, their common opposite. In this manner entitlement and morality, which run through all life spheres, are inappropriately set over against other spheres (family, state) as separate spheres of life, classified along with them. There are in truth two totally different foundations for the distinction: 1. Men have entitlements and duties; 2. Men have both an individual existence and an existence as a member of the objective ethical world structure and of specific organic connections (in both of which they have entitlements and duties). Hegel however unnaturally makes three members out of one distinction, which then is the structure of his legal philosophy. Despite this, the distinction between "morality" and "ethics" does prepare the way, even though in extremely confused fashion, for the proper realization: that *morality is the ethical completion of the individual, while law is the ethical order of the common life of the human race assigned to it* (the people) *as a whole.*

Chapter Two
Positive Law, Natural Law, Revealed Law

§. 10. Law is Positive

As has been explained, law [das Recht] is human order, albeit for the sake of maintaining God's world order (§. 1). It therefore exists as men in a particular time, in a particular country, have established it, and it exists because they *have* so established it, whether good or bad, and not because they in that manner *had* so to establish it, in accordance with a necessity in God's command. This means that law [Recht] is *positive*, but that in the concepts and commandments of the world order of God it has a higher law [Gesetz] to which it *ought* to answer, according to which men *ought* to establish it.[26] Therefore *positive law* [Recht] has over against it a *God-commanded, just, rational* law. Even so, this rational law, the concepts and commandments of God's world order, are not themselves a law [ein Recht] – a so-called *natural law* or *law of reason* – since the essence of law is precisely to be an independent human life order, therefore positive law. Even so, they are the determining [bestimmende] power in positive law, its original ground and archetype, the standard by which it is measured and judged.

---

[26]Regarding morality, no such distinction exists between positive and rational since nowhere does it rest on *human* ordinance but only on God's command. Even mores that are traditional to a certain people, which one might call positive morality, do not bind the individual person in the way positive law does; he is only to follow God's command.

§. 11. Positive Law is Authoritative by Divine Right

God's world order is the archetype of all positive legal construction, but it is not itself a legal construction. Its concepts and commandments, the purpose inhering in life relations, are the principles and the guideline for the laws; but they are not themselves laws by which men in accordance therewith maintain ordered human relations and are able to decide cases of conflict.

For this they firstly are lacking in a determinate shape, the provision of which is the vocation and the freedom of the people. The people themselves, in accordance with the particularity of their spirit and their conditions and with their own creative power, are to give definitive shape to them, to particularize them and thus also to individualize them; and only then do they become applicable norms, or law. The process is similar to the way in which the archetype of the beauty of the human body functions as the guideline which determines the sculptor and by which his sculptures are judged, although itself this archetype is neither a body nor a sculpture with determinate forms and lines which may be cast or sketched. The foundational concepts and relations of the law are in similar manner grounded in God's world order, are divinely necessary, but the specific way in which they are implemented is humanly free – it may be done this way or that way, and therefore it is the way it is, positive. Human freedom is not left simply to sharpen those eternal ideas to a point, so that e.g. positive law need only supply the time interval of prescription or the forms of testament, but it is entrusted with the plan of its realization in general. Thus e.g. property is a concept and commandment in God's world order. Whether however objections [Einrede] or acquisitions can be grounded on a longer period of possession, or whether transfer can occur by contract or only by cession [Uebertragung], or whether the honest buyer must return merchandise without compensation [unentgeldlich herausgeben müsse], even whether the entire institution of property is to be regulated in accordance with the Roman law or with Germanic law, etc., is a free human conception, which although moved and determined by divine commandments nevertheless has its coherence and coordination only in itself. All legal construction therefore has a dual aspect, a divine necessary (natural-law-oriented) and a human free (positive), both permeating each other without dividing line, existing in indissoluble unity.[27]

In the same manner, God's world order is the ground of the regard for law. This human order has a binding power and sanctity only because it serves to uphold that divine order, and because there is truly no law, not even the worst, that does not in some way uphold that order, that is bereft of all reasonableness and justice. Nevertheless, the concepts and commandments of the divine world order have no legal (externally binding) regard in human common life, as long and as far as the human community has not made them into commandments of its order. Only thereby do they become *norms in effect* – laws. This is because the human community is to establish the law as its own life order (§. 1), and it is the human order itself, not the claims on it such as they correspond to the divine order, which has God's sanction externally and commonly to bind men.

---

[27]Already Aristotle (*Ethics*, Book V, ch. 7) divides the content of law (πολιτικόν δίκαιον) into a natural (φυσιαόν) law, which everywhere must be equally in force, and a positive (νομικόν) law that can only be law when it is so established, e.g., the custom of sacrifices in a specific city. However, he sets them up more as externally separated spheres beside each other. By contrast, Melanchthon (*Loci Commune*, p. 229) recognized the proper relation in saying: "Verum quia jus positivum determinatio est juris naturalis, facile intelligi potest, jus positivum tamen habere aliquam regulam, videlicet ne pugnet cum jure naturali." More extensively in Hegel, *Philosophy of Law*, §. 3.

§. 12. Law is Positive Law, not Natural Law

In this manner the human order, which is law, is rooted in the divine; but it is independent in itself, and in this independence consists the *positivity of law*.

The law is *positive in terms of its content*. Although its principles and ideas lie in God's world order, its specific laws are humanly constituted, positive. It is *positive in terms of its validity*. The final ground of its binding regard is God's world order, but the locus of that regard is nevertheless the humanly established order, the existing law. In terms of this independence, the law can even come into conflict with God's world order, which it is to serve; human community, which is called to give the concepts of law a specific shape in accordance with freedom, might turn it into its opposite, ordering the unjust and irrational, and even in this God-opposed makeup the law retains its binding regard. In this the character of *positivity*, which is accorded the law, has its most extreme demonstration.

Law and *positive law* therefore are synonymous terms. There is no other law than positive law. Underlying the idea of a "natural law" are in fact those concepts and commandments of God's world order, the law-ideas [Rechtsideen]; the latter, however, have neither the required specificity, nor the binding power of the law. They are grounds for determination of the further development of the common condition, not norms already in force for the common condition. There are therefore *rational demands* on the law, but there is no *law of reason*. Subjects may not oppose positive law, either as individuals or in the mass, by leaning on natural law; this is the iniquity of the Revolution. The ruling authorities are to uphold the positive law, not the natural law. In particular, the judge is not to pass judgement in accordance with natural law, be it against the positive law, be it only in addition to positive law (subsidiary).

The application of natural law in decisions cannot be realized even factually. It fails in the lack of *objectivity* – common equal recognition – and in the lack of *precision*. The judge would be referred thereby only to his judgement as to what he regards to be natural law, at best he would speak therefore only as an individual (as a mere arbitrator) rather than as a real judge, i.e., as an organ and a representative of national legal judgement, and even with respect to his own judgement he would only find a general legal maxim and not a specific manner of restoring the wrong, which insofar would be arbitrary or based in vague equity.[28]

The application of natural law in the courtroom is however also impermissible legally, is contrary to justice. Every man has the right not to be subjected to any other norm than those which are established as the objective order of the common life, which are sanctioned by the ruling authorities, as the norms of positive law. It does not come into the head of any judge learned in the law to decide in accordance with natural law, be it against, be it outside positive law. Would there have been, prior to recent times when positive law contained laws against unauthorized reprinting, a judge who would find in favor of a lawsuit against reprinting because of natural law? Would there have been a judge in a slave-owning state of North America who recognized a natural right of freedom for

---

[28]The same is true of the general motives or tendencies of legislation, even there, where, inappropriately enough, one has included them in constitutional documents and codes and not merely in their prefaces and declarations of promulgation. For example, "equality before the law," "equality of burdens," "the duty of reimbursement on the part of the state, when by necessity required to sacrifice the rights and advantages of subjects in favor of the common good." Immediate applications of these declarations, in the manner that everywhere is attempted by the participants or by the political parties, must lead to a frightful confusion of the legal condition. The confusions precipitated by the judicial application of that stipulation of the Prussian law code had to be countered with a special law of 1851.

slaves against owners? The rule of natural law instead of or in opposition to positive law has the appearance of establishing the order of God over the order of men: but it is precisely the human order, the law, which is consecrated by God; it is the only common public order that He has ordained over men on earth. The rule of natural law is therefore in truth only the establishment of the arbitrariness of every opinion [Willkür jedweder Meinung] regarding the common public order, it is the establishment of the war of all against all.

§. 13. The Nature of the Case

Something else altogether than so-called natural law (law-ideas) is the *nature of the case* [Natur der Sache]. This designates, not *ethical* (legal) *principles* beyond the principles of positive law, but *factual relations* which afford previously unanticipated, now emphasized bases [Anhaltspunkte] for decisions, precisely in accordance with the *principles of positive law*. So for example our decisions regarding eviction were inferred by Roman jurists from the nature of the case: namely, that because positive law recognizes the binding nature of contracts, liability to vacate an object ensues because of then non-existing right, not because of subsequent events, etc. In the same way, whether newspaper advertisements [Zeitungsinserate] or lithographed orders [lithographirte Bestellungen] by trading houses are to be treated as written documents, whether promises made in a constitutional document have legal consequences, whether in a German state the powers [Befugnisse] of ancient national representative bodies [Landstände] devolve as a matter of course to a contemporary chamber of deputies, all of this can and must be decided in terms of the nature of the case in accordance with positive law, but not according to natural law, to principles of justice outside and alongside positive law.

Something other than so-called natural law are likewise the supreme principles regarding the binding nature of positive law itself, such as that one must obey the ruling authorities, whether there is a limit to obedience and what that limit is, whether active resistance is permissible. All of this is of course not a matter of positive law but exceeds positive law. But it is also not a matter of natural law, but of *morality*, and therefore each man must judge his stance according to his own conscience before God, not in reference to the stance of others, not according to a common public lawful norm (§. 2).

§. 14. Positive Law the Most Immediate Ethical Standard

Accordingly, with regard to the law-ideas – the realization of which is its task – positive law is subject to the standards of *justice, morality, efficiency,* and the like; but it itself, as positive law, is the primary, most immediate ethical measure for the actions of men, and that measure is the standard of *lawfulness* [Rechtmäßigkeit] as opposed to justice and the like. What agrees with positive law is lawful, and vice versa.

§. 15. The Supreme Rule of Legal Development: Continuity

The original condition of the peoples contains the various ethical spheres yet in the compactness of a bud. Law and morality, positive law and the claims of justice on law (natural law) are as yet undistinguished. There exists the simplicity of awareness in which that which is existing law is viewed as just, and that which is just is viewed as existing law. There exists also, however, the fortuitousness, arbitrariness, injustice, of ruling authorities and the judge and the people applying in individual cases that which they hold to be just law, even that which they hold to be moral, without such being established and sanctioned as a general enduring legal order. Therefore it is a desirable advance that the ethical spheres unfold, that law and morality, positive law and the claims of reason on law, step apart in their uniqueness, that positive law, this human order, maintain its full independence, only judged and applied in terms of itself. With the Romans and the Germans – the law peoples par excellence – this development was completed already at the start of their appearance on the stage of world history. Nevertheless, despite this independence, positive law is not to withdraw from the unity of the entire ethical sphere, and the awareness of this unity is not to be eliminated. Even here it is not to be separated from the higher order which it serves. Even in this developed condition, in the nation it is not to pass as something merely human but as the necessary, albeit freely formed, fulfillment of reason and justice, as the maintenance of God's commandments.[29]

In particular, the *continuity* of law serves this purpose, which is why it is the supreme rule of legal development. Continuity does not rule out change and further advance in terms of changed conditions and advancing knowledge; it is not stagnation (stability). On the contrary, it is precisely such advance that is required in order for positive law to gain the recognition of being just and rational. But it requires that all that is new and improved be derived from that which exists, and with all changes in particulars the existing law as a whole never be abolished and another put in its place. Its opposite is the *inco-*

---

[29]So for example, according to eyewitness reports in England the judge in pronouncing sentence on the criminal customarily charges him with meriting such a heavy punishment because he violated God's command. In Germany the judge as a rule will only explain that such and such a section in the civil code prescribes the punishment. In the former case, the human order appears in its unity with God's command; in the latter it is totally separate, as something purely human.

herence [Unzusammenhang] of legal development, the termination of existing legal conditions and erection of new ones by which one switches legislation and chooses among various options thereof, as if that which now exists does not matter to us, in the way one picks and chooses clothing. The former is a development from inside out and therefore gradual, the latter is a change from outside, therefore sudden. In the former case, the legal condition certainly becomes an essentially different one during the course of time, perhaps centuries, and there is no moment in which change can be shown to have taken place; it always maintains its roots in all ages of the history of the people taken together. In the latter case, through a specific occurrence a line is drawn at one fell swoop through the history of the people; what lies beyond that line no longer holds for what lies on this side of that line. The former is the manner of development of all living things; the latter is the manner of treatment of things mechanical. In the former, the plant and the human body grow; in the latter, man changes and exchanges a machine.

Through such continuity of law, the original simplicity of the popular mind, in which that which is existing law is seen as just, that which is just as existing law, is preserved. This is because it effects a situation in which the law in itself is known as none other than the law of the fatherland, by which the existing law in general is considered to be necessary and cannot be otherwise, in spite of many faults in particulars. Against this, the abolition of what is received by picking and choosing among bodies of legislation produces in the public consciousness a complete divorce between what is just and what is positive law. What is just loses its objective existence and exists only in the mind of men, is different for each person; and positive law loses confidence in its necessity and justice. Should the necessity and justice of the existing law be brought into ques-

tion at a fundamental level, in its entirety, then the question
would arise in everyone's mind as to what should be put in the
place of this now abolished legal condition, and, since everything human is questionable, the solution would always be subject to a facile rejection.

§. 16. Revealed Law

God's commandments for the institutions of his world
order (property, family, state) are, as are all of His commandments, partly given in human *conscience*, partly through *God's
revelation* in the Old and New Testaments. That is why in the
elements of law which we set over against positive law we must
consider the revealed commandments to be a special component of the God-given, the reasonable for the human common
condition. The ancients accordingly distinguished between a
positive law, a natural law, and a divine (revealed) law. Even if
we cannot accede to the concept of a revealed law, as little as
to a natural law, there nevertheless exist revealed commandments for the law.

All commands of conscience are likewise corroborated
[bekräftigt] by revelation, and therefore all legal institutions in
their basic concepts likewise are based on revelation, in fact on
the Ten Commandments: "Thou shalt not kill, not steal, not
commit adultery." Therefore only those commands are to be
considered by the law purely to be revealed which are known
to men solely through revelation, or which include a certain
predetermined shape and institution based on a revealed divine
ordinance, such as Sabbath observance, the commandment
regarding divorce, marriage among close relations, institutions
of the church. Accordingly, there is no sharp line drawn between mere commands of conscience (reason) and those given
by revelation.

Even when they are composed clearly and precisely, the commandments of Christian revelation have no immediate validity as law, as little as do the commandments of reason and justice, which likewise are none other than God's commandments. This is based on that one decisive principle: law is the order *established by men*, not the one *called for by God*. One cannot call upon the Holy Scriptures as a legal norm in a court of law; even in the church, one may only refer to the church's understanding of the Holy Scriptures.[30] This is the ground as to why no revealed law exists, as little as does natural law, but only revealed claims on the law.

Against this, the commands of the Christian revelation, like those of reason and justice, form a binding standard for the establishment of law, a claim on the legislator. They are this however in far higher degree and in an entirely different form than the latter because they enjoy the special sanction of God, and because He Himself indicated their particular form, which otherwise is left to human freedom. This is where the claims grounded in revelation (divinum jus) are to be distinguished from those general commandments of justice and reason. This special regard is owed the commandments of the Christian revelation above all because the Christian revelation is the eternal truth, the actual will of God, but furthermore because it is the public faith of the nations of Europe. Christianity cannot refuse obedience to the commandments and declarations of God in the Old and New Testament even in its public institutions without fearfully sinning and contradicting itself.

Certainly, those commandments of revelation are not

---

[30]When e.g. a Catholic clergyman by appealing to Holy Scripture bestows the blessing on the remarriage of innocently divorced spouses, or vice versa when a Protestant clergyman refuses this, the courts and officials of the relevant churches will not uphold the validity thereof.

valid for the *law of Christendom* the purpose of which is only the
sanctification of individual men, such as "he who looks upon a
woman to lust after her commits adultery," "should someone
take your belt, give him your cloak also," and no less those the
purpose of which was for the Jewish nation, such as the
Levirate marriage, the Jewish priesthood. Nevertheless, the
revelation in the Old and New Testaments also contains commandments for Christendom, which therefore has the duty to
maintain them in its common public condition, and thus as
law. So for example regarding divorce or marriage among close
relatives. Which commandments are of this character, which of
that, can only be decided on the merits of each.

§. 17. The Error of Modern Natural Law

The quarrel among the ancients concerning the existence
of a jus naturale as precipitated by Carneades' denial, and
which was again taken up by Grotius in Cicero's train, has to
do with ethics in general and therefore mainly with whether all
mores were introduced merely because of prudence, for the
sake of utility. Only since most recent times, however, does the
struggle date as to whether natural law in our special meaning,
a law derived immediately from reason, exists in distinction to
positive law. Although the objectors in this struggle do recognize subjective ethics (morality), they state that objective ethics
(law) measures up only to the standard of utility. This in opposition to natural law as developed since Grotius. The fact that
no specific decision and no institution stems directly from the
law-ideas of necessity and precisely so arranged leads them to
deny the independence of the law-ideas themselves.

Grotius's entire enterprise however was based on the
error of attempting to discover from the law-ideas that which
is *lawful* rather than that which is appropriate or just (see above,

§. 14). In so doing he performed a signal service for the law of nations, where he did bring norms which were already in observance to clear awareness, and removed doubts as to their obligation. However, regarding natural law, of which he justifiably is viewed as the creator, he created a worthless science. For legal philosophy already existed prior to him, but his science postulated legal philosophy serving also as jurisprudence. Even here, Grotius did the great service of making ideas of *constitutional* law (legal relations between ruling authorities and subjects, etc.) the task of legal philosophy, which hitherto had also been saddled with *political* ideas (expressive perfection [plastische Vollendung] of the state, power, welfare [Wohlstand], mores, etc.). However, he presented these *ideas* behind constitutional law as if they comprised constitutional *law* in general.

Following Grotius, the teachers of natural law posited a concept of natural law as a legal order existing prior to and outside of the state (in the state of nature), continuing in the state alongside positive law, even, as the most consistent among them viewed the matter (Rousseau above all), as an inalienable right of men valid against the state order, so that this latter, when not in agreement with natural law, is null and non-binding. But even among the teachers of positive law, the manner of conceiving the matter became general in the 18th century in which two norms exist for deciding cases, the natural, derived from the natural law (law-ideas), and the positive. The positive law takes precedence where there is a conflict; but in cases where positive law cannot decide, natural law holds as a subsidiary source. One hereby of necessity considered natural law as a self-contained complete body of legislation, on the one hand certainly enriched by positive law but on the other hand richer than positive law. Such a manner of conceptualizing was implemented especially in the then celebrated book of Weber

entitled *Regarding Natural Obligation*. It is also however contained in all the textbooks, such as Thibaut's *Pandects;* it has
even crossed over into legislation, as for example in the Austrian Law Code, which declares natural law to be a subsidiary
source of law in place of the common law, which hitherto has
served that function.

The *Historical School of Law* dropped the entire theory and
it did so implicitly, that is, without taking precise account of
the ground as to why one may deny the validity of the law of
reason, without asking whether positive law is entirely arbitrary, whether in so doing one denies all absolute ethical standard for the law, leaving only the relative standard of suitability
to people, time and conditions. Considerations of the latter
sort are supposed of the Historical School, and they might be
harbored by many of its supporters wishing to put right their
relationship to the earlier viewpoint. Nevertheless, these supporters are entirely oblivious to the true spirit of this school,
which consists much rather in a *direct pervasion of the recognition of
the positiveness of law*, as it has here been attempted to deduce
from philosophical principles.

In life itself, the concept of *positive law* – that is, the sole
validity of norms established in the common life of the nation,
to the exclusion of those derived from ethical motives or mere
law-ideas – was first realized in the Roman era, just as the
Romans were the first to realize the concept of *acquired rights*
and their inviolability. The law, both in its objective and subjective signification, consequently there appears for the first
time in world history in its pure form as an independent sphere
of life. This is why the Romans justifiably are considered to be
the classic people in the cause of civil order.

Any validity for "natural law" is therefore least of all to
be sought among the Romans. Even so, their terminology can
easily lead to misunderstanding. For them, "jus naturale"

signified the component of law necessary by nature, not an embodiment of legal principles; jus gentium, that portion of positive law which contained generally observed legal determinations, not those peculiar to Rome, which therefore were accustomed to be seen to have come from general law-ideas (naturalis ratio), not however a law separate from positive law, which might be derived immediately from the law-ideas.

Chapter Three
The Origin and Sources of Law

§. 18. Human Community as the Source of Law

The way in which law arises is commensurate with its essence, to wit, the human order of the common condition for
the maintenance of God's world order. Law arises through the
human community, through the people and ruling authorities,
but with the consciousness of a necessity and an authorization
in God's order – either through establishment by the ruling
authorities, since they have the vocation from God to maintain
order – *through statute*, or through *observance among the people* with
the consciousness that a norm is part of the legal order to
which one is subject from God – through *custom* [Gewohnheit]
and *tradition* [Herkommen].

The law thus proceeds from the people as an originally
given unity, either through uniform regard for the ruling authorities or through the uniform consciousness of the people,
which above all fills everyone and determines their actions; not
from individual men who then first come together in order to
establish the law in mutual agreement.

The law arises from the awareness to fulfill a commandment of God (or, where faith in God is lacking, to fulfill an
ethical necessity) to which man is bound, and not as an arbitrary institution or for mere human protection and utility. For
this reason the people's ethical valuation of life determines the
law's content, and it therefore arises originally, apart from
choice or predetermination [Absicht], out of a direct impression of necessity, which preponderantly determines even the
regulations of the ruling authorities *(principle of the Historical*

School). Now free reflection as to what is just or unjust, and the
consideration of utility and salubrity, immediately manifests
itself, and this free activity expands with advancing culture.
Nevertheless, it remains reflection on the basis of the immediate ethical and legal judgement of the nation, the consideration
of utility remaining ever rooted in the ground of the commandments of justice; and the entire law-developing action,
even in free reflection and consideration of utility, is permeated
with the sentiment of duty and the principles and commandments given beyond human choice.

The law arises first through establishment as external
order in the life of the community. The mere consciousness of
law among the people does not yet have the binding power of
law until it is transferred to external life, there coming to expression and form. The will of the ruling authorities must be
proclaimed in a determinate form, the legal conception
[Ansicht] of the people must be activated [bethätigt] in custom
in order to become law. Legal consciousness is only the power
and action [Wirksamkeit] of God's requirements in the soul,
and, like these requirements themselves (the law-ideas), it does
not yet ground any law. First this establishment in external life,
which is the act of men, grounds the human order, which is
the concept of law. First this establishment produces the common external shape of life (objective ethos), which is the concept of law. The law thus established as external objective order then separates itself from the grounds of its origin into an
independent existence. It is not valid *as* the will of the ruling
authorities or *as* the popular consciousness, but only *as* law.
God's order inheres in the external objective order as such,
which is to support it. For this reason the law remains no less
in force even when the legal consciousness of the people and
the ruling authorities has long become something else, when
everyone considers the law to be irrational and unjust, and,

with regard to valid legal norms, when one no longer even considers their origin; in fact, they gain in sanctity to the degree that such awareness sinks into oblivion.

Such a transition from inward valuation to external *establishment* and validity is the concept of the *sources of law*, and accordingly in general there are only two sources: *custom* and *legislation*, i.e., observance as law, and establishment by authority.

§. 19. The Two Sources of Law: Custom and Legislation

Custom is determination for the *popular* consciousness, i.e., the consciousness of the people who abide by the law, and insofar as they do so – be it only the high nobility; custom therefore concerns the necessity of *observance* of a legal rule (opinio necessitatis).

Legislation is determination for the *governmental* consciousness, i.e., the consciousness of those whose vocation is to establish the law – be it only the democratic assembly; legislation hence concerns the necessity of the *introduction* of a legal rule in accordance with justice or utility.

Custom thus rests on an immediate legal judgement, legislation on a reflected-upon (legal-philosophical or political) judgement. The content of custom is therefore derived from that legal consciousness that fills the community as ethical substance, as a determining inclination; the content of legislation comes from deliberation and the will of certain persons, based on the foundation of that consciousness. With the former, establishment in external life follows from the gradual ongoing subjection of conduct; with the latter, it comes through a sort of command. The former is the organic manner of gradual unobservable emergence, analogous to mores and language, while the latter is the manner of the mind, of personality, emergence out of predetermination through action in a specific moment. For that reason the subject of customary law is *natural* communities: area, rank, people; the subject of legislation is *legally constituted* (i.e., fashioned into an acting personality) communities: municipality, corporation, state.

In consequence, law exercises its power over men immediately in custom, in legislation by means of the human authorities sanctioned by the law itself, and therefore through free human establishment. It corresponds to man's twofold position as *creature* and as *personality* that human community first has law as a given reality over itself, and then, on the basis of this given reality, it establish law over itself through its own action. The former given reality is customary law. Its legal rules have established themselves through their own inherent power over consciousness; they were not decided upon by any man and are not supported by any regard for those rules, but are valid in themselves. The legal rules of legislation, however, are introduced by men and are valid because of regard for their originator [Urheber]. This removes the objection made against customary law as to how subjects can bind others through their previous actions. It is not regard for *them* which binds later generations, but regard for the power which continually determines men in their actions independently of each other, and for the rule and order which they hereby establish in their inner valuation and external life. The persons through whose observance custom is developed are not the originators but only the medium of customary law.

Customary law accordingly by no means rests on a concession of the legislator; it is an independent, in fact the original source of law. For legislation itself presupposes customary law, since an immediately given law must already exist for there to be legal authorities, by means of which it from that point arises. The entire constitution [Alle Verfassung], thus the legislative power itself, is originally customary law. But legislation certainly enjoys a higher regard in that it includes in its concept free rule over the encountered legal order. The legislator therefore has the power to abolish custom or to cut it off in advance to the degree that he factually penetrates to that end [so weit er thatsächlich damit durchdringt].[31] At any rate, to the degree that he can prohibit and does not do so he is the cause of customary law, albeit a negative, not a positive one.

§. 20. The Binding Power of Customary Law

In accordance with its origin and seat, the binding power of customary law lies in both aspects: the legal consciousness (opinio necessitatis) and observance in consequence thereof. The latter apart from the former is meaningless; but likewise the former without the latter has no validity, is not yet law (see §. 11). Custom as such is therefore by no means a mere characteristic, or the "irrefutable witness of a law which arose prior to it and from elsewhere," "so that the origin of law is independent of custom," but an aspect of the origin and binding power of the law that is just as necessary as legal consciousness itself. This is analogous to how the criminal will and the criminal act are both equally essential aspects of crime. Both, inner consciousness and outer realization, must be in evidence in the entire legal sphere, in accordance with its character as external ethos.

The binding power of legislation however has its seat in the lawful regard for the legislator and the proclamation of his will (promulgation – Royal Assent).

The ground of this binding power is however the same for both: and that is the *regard for the law* itself, i.e., the given external order over men. Legal norms arise through custom, in that through it they become elements of this existing order

---

[31]For example, the Austrian Code, §. 10.

(and indeed it is not the origin of custom but its continuance [Bestand] that is the basis of its validity) and through legislation, in that they proceed from the authority which the existing order designates. It is therefore not the national conviction or the national will which is the ground of the binding power of the law; it is much rather the law which is the ground by which the national will binds individuals, and the manner in which it does so. To ground the regard for law on the national conviction is analogous to grounding moral laws on conscience. Law, like morality, has the ground of its binding power absolutely in itself, but in accordance with its peculiar character it has this power not merely in its idea but likewise in its external continuance [Bestande]. In terms of its provenance it is a potential in the nation, while in terms of its continuance and its validity a power over it. The national conviction therefore is certainly the source of the determinate content of the law, and the necessary means by which it comes to its external, objective existence. But the ground of the regard for law does not lie in that national conviction but in law's own ethical power, which in fact effected that national conviction, and in its existence, mediated through this and no less through outward establishment, although now having become independent. In this independent existence it passes through the generations, without any of them being able to lay claim to it as its work, as the order over the nation which connects the nation and the ages.

The regard for the legislator therefore is not based on the fact that he is the organ and representative of the national conviction but that he is the organ of the law and its power over the nation. The consequence of the opposing viewpoint would be for customary law and legislation continuously having to measure up to the national conviction, with their validity dependent upon the verdict regarding their correspondence. The teaching of the Historical School in its innermost motive does not consist in deriving the *validity* of the law from the popular *will*, but in deriving the *content* of the law from the popular *consciousness*.[32] Its intention is not to set persons, the people, over the law, but on the contrary to put persons and therefore also the legislator under the law, that is, its development in national history. The subjectivity principle, to which such an error belongs, has however ensconced itself so deeply in the culture [Bildung] of the times that in its expression it perhaps every so often brushes on the same thing [mitunter nahe an denselben hinstreift].

In the final analysis it is the power of God's world order which produces the law and lends it its regard. It moves the peoples and their ruling authorities to establish norms which in greater or lesser degree answer to it and which for that reason they recognize to be that which is just, rational, worthwhile [gebotenen]. It is the ground of the regard for ruling authorities and therefore for the binding power of the laws. It is also the true and reasonable [einleuchtende] ground of the binding power of custom; because it is that which, as an awareness of constraint (opinio necessitatis), determines the actions of men. Regard for *it*, not regard for observing men nor for the popular view [Volksansicht], consecrates custom, which has arisen out of the awareness to obey it. This has nothing to do with an "immediate connection of law with the divine will." The law derives its content immediately from the national consciousness and its regard immediately from itself. But its final ground lies in a higher order of the ethical world, which is nothing other than the commandment of the living personal God. Thusly does law lend itself to religious faith, which does not deceive. Thus also must true science understand it. Since no ethical power is possible apart from a living subject, if one sep-

---

[32]This is a frequent misunderstanding. In such confusion, Gönner attributes to Savigny a democratic tendency.

arates the law from God one gives it the people for its subject, no longer treating it as law but as national conviction, and the eternal divine content of the law comes to be considered mutable according to people, time and conditions, and to be at man's disposal.

§. 21. The Wrongheadedness of Codification

In accordance with the dual position from which they arise (see §. 19), both manners of law's origin, custom and legislation, are always necessary, each with its own particular value and own sphere of application.

Custom has the merit of greater venerableness,[33] the undoubted merit of legal consciousness entirely unmolested by the possibility of something else, and, in the initial shape it gives to the legal condition, also of greater harmony. This is because nature always works more harmoniously than reflection. Legislation for its part is a higher attestation of the human spirit and has the merit of freedom and reflection, and thus the greater power of correction, direction toward purposes, and greater precision and forcefulness.

Custom thus develops the legal condition *originally* and in its *totality*. It arises together with life relations themselves and provides them with the norm; it makes them into legal relations. Legislation then enters the picture. When a situation presents itself to legislation's scrutiny, as a rule it has already for some time been taken hold of by that invisible constructing power of law and brought to a certain level of development. Scrutiny is precipitated, partly by contradiction between law

---

[33]Thus Aristotle (*Politics* III. 11): "Ἔτι κυριώτεροι καὶ περὶ κυριωτέρων τῶν κατὰ γράμματα νόμων οἱ κατὰ τὰ ἔθη εἰσίν." In the same manner Lycurgus prohibited the writing of the laws.

which arose in past times and the conditions or the values of the present, partly through immediately present need (because for a newly arisen relation often no corresponding observance has been developed, especially pertaining to those relations resting more on utility than justice), and partly, finally, by purposes for the future. For the purpose [Sinn] of the ruling authorities, the outflow of which is legislation, is toward arranging [Absicht], guidance [Lenkung] and direction toward goals [Richtung für Zwecke]; legislation therefore does not restrict itself to providing the seal of approval to already developed life relations but also has the vocation to call forth future life relations primarily by means of institutions in a creative and intuitive [divinirend] manner (Beseler).

Certainly, custom remains at all times a fertile [ergiebige] source both for the new production of law and for the further advance of the written law; in the period of higher consciousness and freer reflection, however, legislation must engross a greater sphere over against it, and the higher the degree of systematic character the law gains, the more it must itself increase in consciousness. Therefore when one demands that law's conditions grow in a gradual unconscious manner, in the manner of the middle ages, one opposes the principle of our time. Despite this, the legislator in no way takes the place originally occupied by custom: he may not undertake to create the legal condition *starting anew and in its entirety.* For human freedom is not absolutely creative.[34]

This yields the assessment regarding *codification.* By codification one understands the composition of law *codes*

---

[34]Man of course possesses an unlimited power to destroy in accordance with free reflection, but only a limited power so to build. For instance, how difficult would it be for us to produce a constitution according to the Greek manner or on the basis of medieval feudal principles! Even the French Revolution, with its apparent absolute free reflection, was locked into an extremely small circle of specific concepts.

which are intended to contain the *total law*, be it for a specific area of life (civil constitution [Civil-Verfassung]), be it even for the entire public condition (e.g., the Prussian Law Code). It is the extreme form of legislation. It provides the legal condition with an entirely different character. Originally and up to that point, the legal condition of all peoples rests in its entirety on custom, which supports and encompasses it. A few more or less comprehensive laws are added to this, which in their place intervene in that entirety, which date from various times and collectively [sämmtlich], the earlier and the later, are independent of each other. With codification, however, the legal condition is based in its entirety on the code, which supports and encompasses it. Custom is only a mere exception within the code, but individual laws are likewise mere exceptions. Laws dating back to before the code are no longer valid; laws dating from afterward appear as appendices ["Novellen"] to the code, and when they begin to mount, one treats it as an invitation to a new codification.

Thus by means of codification the legal condition in its entirety is based on statute instead of custom, on the work of human reflection rather than on the drive to develop given by nature. This of necessity entails the disadvantage on the one hand that given the restriction of human reflection and perspective, even with the most successful implementation a significant incongruity remains with real life and its requirements; and on the other hand that continuity, the historical unity of the legal condition, is broken, divided into a before and after the Codex, by which the awareness of necessity, which to that point was on the side of the existing law, gives way to the notion of arbitrary selecting and changing (§. 15). For this reason codification is an unnatural, a bad form of legal condition.

This does not mean that all codes under all circumstances are to be rejected. They might be justified by way of exception following profound shocks and uprootings, upon wholesale changes in life relations or mores which perhaps over longer periods of time had remained unaccounted for, upon actual and not merely presumed confusion in existing legal material, a confusion which in fact arises most easily through legislation itself.[35] They are also less questionable in spheres which merely regulate the actions of state power than in those which regulate the life relations of the people, e.g., less so for procedural or criminal law than for civil law or above all for constitutional law, and are most appropriate for certain relations involving a less deep ethical relation and with those concerning which agreement across the entire nation is desirable, such as the law relating to bills of exchange. Beyond that, its profitableness depends on the historical and systematic insight of the age and on the possession of persons sufficiently gifted for the work, who, like geniuses in art, are not born every day. Under all conditions, the first step from the historical form of legal condition to that of the code remains extremely hazardous and should not be taken except in extreme necessity.

However, even where codes seem appropriate and even indispensable, they should, to the degree possible within this form, retain the *continuity of the legal condition*. Accordingly, the legislator firstly should not change the received *structure* of the law, that is, the legal concepts, without need and clear awareness, even when he must change legal provisions. This holds

---

[35]"But if laws heaped upon laws shall swell to such a vast bulk, and labor under such confusion as renders it expedient to treat them anew, and reduce them into one sound and serviceable corps, it becomes a work of the utmost importance, deserving to be deemed heroical, and let the authors of it be ranked among legislators, and the restorers of states and empires." Sir Francis Bacon, *The Advancement of Learning*, edited by Joseph Devey (New York: P.F. Collier and Son, 1901 [1605]), book VIII, ch.3, aphor. 59.

equally for individual statutes and for entire codes. A new
structure which does away with the past voids, in terms of result, the entire received legal condition, because although it
appears to have stayed the same, in fact it has changed into
something else, since in the new relation it realizes a new effect.
This total change in legal content does not lie within the purpose of legislation; even with codification, such a purpose
much rather extends only to secure command of that content
and to examination [Sichtung] and improvement in details. It is
entirely ungrounded, for real life has no need for it. It leads to
confusion, because the relation of the new to the old cannot be
overlooked; and finally it makes it impossible to utilize earlier
experiences because it has changed precisely the conditions
which they had undergone. Rather than truly sifting in order to
eliminate the faulty and discordant, every legislation in this
manner becomes an entirely new experiment.[36]

And another thing: the legislator is not to *annul in principle*
previous law, even where he formulates the legal condition
newly in systematic form, but, to the degree that it is not either
directly or indirectly definitively abolished, to allow it to con-

---

[36]So for example Justinian in the *Const. De transform. usucap.* and in
the *Nov.* 115 entirely wisely and appropriately changed the legal provisions
but, without knowing or wanting to, also changed or, as the case may be,
confounded the legal concepts (of usucapio, praescriptio, nullity [Nullität],
unduteousness [Inofficiosität], etc.), thus producing highly disadvantageous
confusion. How totally must this be the case when entire codes take that
course! In the transition from old to new legal conditions, knots should be
untied rather than cut through, which is why the vocation for new codes
requires historical and systematic insight in the existing law. For this reason
Savigny's book *On the Vocation of Our Time for Legislation and Legal Science* [see
note, p. 3 above – RCA] mainly assumes the lack of insight into the structure
of existing law and by extension the danger of producing a new edition. By
no means does it oppose material reform. That such a lack of insight truly
existed at that time, and not merely in terms of degree, and thus susceptible
of infinite improvement, but in its very nature, has adequately been demonstrated through the insight attained since then.

tinue in force. This is not a mere *subsidiary* validity, the kind which one can likewise attribute to a foreign received law, but *immanent* validity, as existing in the continuity of the legal condition; accordingly, former law does not find its application merely in the areas in which the new law is silent but also in those in which new law speaks, as the explanation [Erklärung] and root of that law, along with it and in it. The principled abolition of existing law in order to put into force only that which is contained in the new code leads at once to material shortcoming, since no human legislator is capable of exhausting life.[37] Hence, it destroys the unity of the national law and legal consciousness. Instead of the further development from its original national foundation [Anlage] being continuously preserved, as in the case of that immanent validity of previous law, here all future effect is founded simply on the coincidental viewpoint of a specific point in time and a specific individual who happens to be the legislator. Finally, it cuts off from the legal system [Rechtswesen] the fruit of the scientific might and achievements which were attached to the preceding; this is especially grievous with regard to the new civil legislation, because it is precisely in the area of civil law that the most illustrious achievements are rooted in the classical common law. The more the codes in this manner fundamentally and in point of fact grant validity to the pre-existing [vorgefundenen], naturally grown and historical law, the less they fall under the strict definition of codification, and the more they retain the charac-

---

[37]So for example the Bavarian constitution arranged nothing for the *apanage* [provision for the subsistence of royal descendants – RCA] in the case of a prince of the blood ascending to a foreign throne. When this case came up, there were no grounds for decision in accordance with the codification principle. In terms of the principle of ongoing validity of past [vergangenen] law, however, grounds were available in the *nature of the apanage*, as contained not in the constitution but in never-destroyed German constitutional law [deutsche Staatsrecht] and in historical precedents.

ter of simply more extensive statutes. The degree to which this is possible and profitable depends on the circumstances which brought on the necessity of the code in the first place.

This then is the criticism of the newer codification, that the procedure associated with it is the opposite of all of that. Codification per se is considered the normal, the higher sort of arrangement of the law, and one therefore needlessly resorts to it, merely for the sake of the excellence of this form, in order for the entire law to be a consciously thought-out work of men, in order for the present purely to stand on its own, divorced from the past. One furthermore approaches the matter by treating existing law not as binding and determinative – questioning, without having a practical need to, whether better material determinations exist than those which it contains, giving it a new structure, taking away its entire validity, annulling everything not contained in the code. Instead of bringing the received legal condition to clear awareness, reforming where needed, one much rather destroys it in order to put an entirely new one in its place. Here the purpose is not to create the *content* of the law a priori by reason – one has for the most part come back on this error – but to ground the *validity* of all law a priori on the new code, referring the people and the jurists simply to the code, so that in a manner of speaking the existence of the law first dates from the code. Apart from all these negative consequences, this in itself degrades [an sich eine Heruntersetzung der] the *sanctity of the law*, while it no longer is treated as a power existing from nature, only passing through the legislative act, but rather in its entirety is treated as a product of the human action of legislation.[38]

---

[38]Much new legislation has furthermore gone astray by construing legal principles themselves a priori as a philosophical system, or to define them as in a textbook. The definitions then become for it not only a negative, the border guard, which keeps out certain things it wishes to exclude,

A form of code that does not interfere quite as much as this is the *corpus* [Sammlung], examples of which are Justinian's Codex and the Decretals of Gregory XI. Here previous laws are listed in their own original form and on the strength of their own original authority. Hence it is not based on the principle that the entire law is first sanctioned *today*, and the requirement exists neither systematically to fill out the entire sphere of law nor theoretically to examine every rule now for the first time [jetzt erst]. To do this the corpus lacks that principled inner motive [Beweggrundes]; it is virtually solely oriented toward the external goal of facilitating usage, and therefore in no way can serve as an example for us.

Another form of code to be distinguished from codification is the *register* [Aufzeichnung] of previous law, either combined with significant reform qua content or not. It indeed proclaims all its laws as new and sanctioned for the first time by itself – this in contradistinction to the corpus – but it is not conceived as a conclusive and therefore exhaustive [schlies-

---

and of which it therefore is conscious; but it aims thereby to exhaust the matter itself, and everything it does not include in the definition – those things of which it is not aware, as well as those things it excludes consciously – is stripped of juridical consequences. Instead of e.g. pointing out the concepts of robbery, of theft, burglary as the nation and the jurists have done so in accordance with practice up until now, and only to guard against what it recognizes as a specific shortcoming, either of an overly narrow or an overly broad formulation, or where it fears confusion with a related concept, it much rather constructs these living facts from categories and characteristics, and only accepts that which it fortuitously has comprehended thereby as theft, as robbery, as burglary. There will then certainly be cases which do not fit these characteristics and nevertheless truly constitute such crimes. And when legislation considers it necessary to teach e.g. what burglary is, let's say the violent forcing of a repository [etwa gewaltsame Erbrechung eines Behältnisses], it will, if it is consistent, not be able to leave it to human consciousness to decide what is violent, what is forcing, what is a repository; it will have to keep on going with its establishment of concepts until, as in Hegel's philosophy, it arrives at the definition of pure empty being.

sendes und darum erschöpfendes] system. Hence it is the form in which historical continuity as stipulated above is maintained. An example of this is given in the Twelve Tables legislation. Although extending across the entire area of law, it laid no claim to cover it and, to the degree that it did not, it left room for the old norms. Just so the Law of Moses, to the degree that it concerned secular relations; no less so the most ancient codes of the Germanic peoples. This manner of composition is just as applicable at our level of scientific advance and is truly the appropriate one.

§. 22. The Role of Legal Science and Court Practice

Legal science has the task of bringing the law to complete and systematic awareness in order to apply it either to future rules (*theory*) or to obtain judgement regarding an existing case (*praxis*). Its activity is to discover customs [die Gewohnheiten aufzufinden] and to delimit them in sharp outline, as well as to interpret the laws, and regarding both, to discover the underlying principles from which to gain new legal rules, to grasp [erfassen] the system of the whole law [gesammten Rechts], i.e., its mutual interlocking [Ineinanderschliessen] to form a total effect [Totalwirkung], and to arrange its application in terms of that spirit. It thereby brings the latent content of the law to full and harmonious development.[39] In this manner it is truly productive; it is an element of legal development, no less fertile than custom and statute, but in no way original and independent the way they are, rather ever dependent upon a given reality before it, so that its results are continually to be measured in terms of agreement with that reality. The class [Stand] which in more mature times has the special vocation of

[39]Puchta has exceptionally concisely formulated the meaning of legal science in his *Pandects*, 2nd ed., §. 16.

performing this function in no way does so as representative of the popular conviction, as little as does the legislator (see §. 20), but as representative of the law, this higher power over the people. Hence it is due to the necessity of the law and not to the representation of popular opinion that because this or that principle is valid for the legal condition, the proper [sachgemässe] development of it must be valid, and that that which has been determined in consequence of legal application is valid as a component of the existing legal order.[40]

The harmonious development of legal content and its principles to their full extent, covering all of life, is accordingly a scientific and not a governmental vocation, and to desire that the legislative power take care of this is a mistaken usage thereof. Where the necessary norms can be derived from existing principles, one should not pass a law but rather refer jurists to their own scientific activity. It is a mechanical conception of this day and age that a law must always be thought up in this manner, and it was not the least of the accomplishments of the Historical School to combat this mechanical conception. How excellent are the principles in Roman law regarding eviction, accident [Zufall], negligence [Fahrlässigkeit], compensation for damages [Schadensersatz bei der Vindikation], etc., which were gained purely through scientific activity without any help from legislation! But then legal science cannot replace legislation. Only legislation may make independent isolated decrees [Anordnungen] or wholly new principles and living arrange-

---

[40]Puchta's designation of the legal profession [Juristenstandes] as "representative of the people," and similarly Savigny's, does not have the significance of its being the representative of the laity and its convictions, but that it is the bearer of a national vocation and therefore in this is the bearer and true representative of the national consciousness (see above, §. 18). This rebuts the objection that in consequence of this designation the learned law [Juristenrecht] must first be measured against the popular (read: lay) conviction.

ments [Lebesgestaltungen], or do away with [Ausstossung] valid ordinances.

Giving legal science full play therefore is not in conflict with legislation according to its true vocation. It is just as little in conflict with the influence which is continually exercised by the popular consciousness, and therefore custom, on legal formation. For the latter is able originally to produce norms, while legal science can only systematically assimilate existing ones. That legal science, like every specialized activity and no less legislation, might detach itself from the collective spirit of the nation and become one-sided does not abrogate its natural [naturgemäss] significance, but it may render institutions desirable which reduce this danger, as long as such are otherwise capable of being implemented and profitable.

Legal science finds its transition into life *indirectly* in many ways, through custom and legislation, in that it determines the viewpoint of the people and the ruling authorities; *directly* however through *court practice* [Gerichtsgebrauch], that is, the even-handed application of a norm by the courts [Gerichte]. In this manner the courts become the actual organ, i.e., means of determination, for legal science, in the way custom is for the popular consciousness and statutes are for the will of the ruling authorities.[41] As ongoing observance of a norm in the awareness of already existing obligation (opinio necessitatis), it is a species [Gattung] of customary law in the broader sense. Nevertheless, it has its own unique character, in that the legal valuation from which it springs is a *legal-scientific* judgement in the broadest sense, or a *juridical* judgement, that is, a judgement

---

[41]A legal perspective of the people can certainly be established by court practice, it being likewise the organ for this, but always mediately, through the activity of jurists (administering justice [Rechtssprechenden]), which, as is shown below, absolutely has a legal-scientific character in the broadest sense.

regarding the validity of a norm *on the basis of principle* and in coherence with the *whole law*, be it a legally expert judgement [rechtskundiges Urtheil], that is, a judgement as to whether a legal norm (namely custom) already exists, as occurred with the ancient lay assessors [Schöffen], or be it a *true legal-scientific* judgement, that is, one in which the legal norm is to be derived from the existing law. A legal-scientific function nonetheless underlies the former, be it ever so imperceptibly, namely in the substantiation [Begründung] of the norm, particularly e.g. custom, through conscious conclusions [Schlüsse] gained from observances, and the specification of the norm with regard to the remainder of the law. This decisively characterizes the standpoint of the judiciary over against the standpoint of the people, out of which custom arises. Custom is the consciousness of subjection under a norm, immediate and isolated. The binding power of court practice therefore is based on the general ground of customary law, viz. gradual establishment in the external order, but it has a special character in accordance with its peculiar nature.

Since in fact court practice is the outflow of a legal-scientific judgement, which for its part, in accordance with the above, has a given reality ever before it against which it always is examined, the validity of court practice is also dependent upon this examination to the degree that such legal-scientific judgements exist in ongoing application, e.g., court practice regarding the three degrees of fault [culpa].[42] Should however

---

[42]**culpa**: Fault, neglect, negligence. A term in civil law, meaning fault, neglect, or negligence. There are three degrees of *culpa*: *lata culpa*, gross fault or neglect; *levis culpa*, ordinary fault or neglect; *levissima culpa*, slight fault or neglect, and the definitions of these degrees are precisely the same as those in our law.

This term is to be distinguished from *dolus*, which means fraud, guile, or deceit.

From *Robertson's Words for a Modern Age: A Dictionary of Latin and Greek Words used in Modern English Vocabulary*, available on the Internet at

court practice be detached from the juristic operation that evoked it, and should this be lost to consciousness so that the practice in the end appears as something independent, it then acquires unconditional power (legis vicem); for example, the court practice that *pacta* are actionable or that a compensation payment [Genugthuungssumme] can be claimed [gefordert] from an engagement of marriage [Verlöbnis]. This occurs of necessity and in short order[43] where jurists follow a custom or are determined [bestimmt] by an immediate need of life [Lebensbedürfniss]; but even where they attain that result through mediated scientific activity, even perhaps through historical misunderstanding, it could arrive at that, as for example in our summary procedure regarding possessory interdicts. Here then court practice differs fundamentally from custom, which has unconditional validity since popular consciousness, the organ of which it is, is an immediate element of legal generation [Rechtserzeugung] which undergoes no further examination.

On the other hand, however, there is a special consideration attending to court practice: for the sake of both legal certainty [Rechtssicherheit] and seemliness [des Anstandes willen], every court must be in agreement with itself. For this reason court practice, already in the stage in which it began to develop, enjoyed a certain degree of regard while custom did not, as long as it was not fully developed and settled [entschieden]. To wit, *precedents* [Präjudicien] and *praxis* are to be distin-

---

http://www.wordinfo.info – RCA.

[43]Precisely this result is based by Savigny in the presumption of a twofold sort of court practice, one being the same thing as actual custom, and by Puchta in distinguishing two sorts of juristic activity, with jurists in their immediate judgement, as the representatives of the popular conviction, being unconditional sources of law, while in their legal-scientific judgement always being subject to scrutiny. In accordance with my entire conception of law, I cannot evade also attributing a significance to established court practice as such.

guished, i.e., individual observable occurrences [Vorgänge] as opposed to lengthy continuous application usually no longer capable of being accounted for. The former is incipient, the latter settled, established court practice.[44] Mere praxis is capable of attaining to unconditional validity (legis vicem) in accordance with the above-mentioned preconditions. But a court shall not deviate from its precedents even in cases of doubt. Beyond this, the regard for precedents can be intensified through positive law and in consequence of national organization (high-court rules of procedure [gemeine Bescheide] – Prussian and Bavarian law regarding precedents).

§. 23. The Role of Court Practice in the Generation of Law

And so the elements of legal generation are popular consciousness, the purpose of the ruling authority, and legal science. The *sources of law* in the technical sense however are custom, legislation, court practice. It is imprecise to count legal science as a source of law. For the concept of the sources of law designates the bases or organs through which legal rules

---

[44]Thus for example our bankruptcy procedure rests on praxis, not precedents. Furthermore, cf. Bacon, *op. cit.*, aphor. 95 and 96 [95. If judgment be given upon a case in any principal court, and a like case come into another court, proceed not to judgment before a consultation be held in some considerable assembly of the judges. For if decrees are of necessity to be cut off, at least let them be honorably interred. 96. For courts to quarrel and contend about jurisdiction is a piece of human frailty, and the more, because of a childish opinion, that it is the duty of a good and able judge to enlarge the jurisdiction of his court; whence this disorder is increased, and the spur made use of instead of the bridle. But that courts, through this heat of contention should on all sides uncontrollably reverse each other's decrees which belong not to jurisdiction, is an intolerable evil, and by all means to be suppressed by kings, the senate, or the government. For it is a most pernicious example that courts, which make peace among the subjects, should quarrel among themselves. – RCA.]

obtain validity, not those through which they arise in consciousness. A source of law is only the statute [das Gesetz] and that which has the force of law ("legis vicem obtinet"). This cannot however be said of legal science. The doctrine of legal science as such (communis opinio) is simply incapable of obtaining binding regard from the judge since it lacks that establishment in the external order, just as little as does the popular consciousness. Only court practice, which does embody such establishment, is capable of this under the above-mentioned conditions.[45] It is entirely appropriate to construe those elements of legal generation and the sources of law corresponding to them (their manner of establishment) in their unity and accordingly to designate them as elements of the total legal condition: popular law [Volksrecht], learned law [Juristenrecht], and legislation. But one must guard himself from the error of considering the aspects of popular consciousness and of legal science detached from custom and independently established court practice.

The external determination of the law, which resulted from its nature as common external life arrangement (objective ethos), therefore is everywhere just as essential an element as is the national consciousness from which it springs. It is that which is the seat of law's independent power, detached from the national consciousness and its vagaries. Therefore among all true law-peoples prior practice is held in high esteem already as such, apart from its inner reasons. Among the Romans, this

---

[45]When positive laws grant force of law to legal science, in so doing they make certain jurists into judges, similar to the councils of law professors [Spruchkollegien (bodies of university law professors who provided courts with legal opinions – RCA)] (responsa prudentum) or certain writings on codes (Citiredikt) – but they do not make legal science as such into a source of law. Maurenbrecher (De auct. jurisprud.) reckons the opinio jurisc. to be a source of law in that he puts legal scholars on a level with judges, through the erroneous presupposition that the regard for court practice rests on judges being legal scholars.

was true of everything which had become tralatitium; among the English, the precedents.[46] In its independent existence,

---

[46]Bacon, *op. cit.*, aphor. 21 ff. ["Precedents and the Use of Forms": 21. We come next to precedents; from which justice may be derived where the law is deficient, but reserving custom, which is a kind of law, and the precedents which, through frequent use, are passed into custom, as into a tacit law; we shall at present only speak of such precedents as happen but rarely, and have not acquired the force of a law, with a view to show how and with what caution a rule of justice may be derived from them when the law is defective. 22. Precedents are to be derived from good and moderate times, and not from such as are tyrannical, factious, or dissolute; for this latter kind are a spurious birth of time, and prove more prejudicial than instructive. 23. Modern examples are to be held the safest. For why may not what was lately done, without any inconvenience be safely done again? Yet recent examples have the less authority; and, where things require a restoration, participate more of their own times than of right reason. 24. Ancient precedents are to be received with caution and choice; for the course of time alters many things; so that what seems ancient, in time may, for disturbance and unsuitableness, be new at the present; and therefore the precedents of intermediate times are the best, or those of such times as have most agreement with the present, which ancient times may happen to have more than later. 25. Let the limits of a precedent be observed, and rather kept within than exceeded; for where there is no rule of law, everything should be suspected: and therefore, as this is a dark road, we should not be hasty to follow. 26. Beware of fragments and epitomes of examples, and rather consider the whole of the precedent with all its process; for if it be absurd to judge upon part of a law without understanding the whole, this should be much rather observed of precedents, the use whereof is precarious, without an evident correspondence. 27. It is of great consequence through what hands the precedents pass, and by whom they have been allowed. For if they have obtained only among clerks and secretaries, by the course of the court, without any manifest knowledge of their superiors; or have prevailed among that source of errors, the populace, they are to be rejected or lightly esteemed. But if they come before senators, judges, or principal courts, so that of necessity they must have been strengthened, at least by the tacit approval of proper persons, their dignity is the greater. 28. More authority is to be allowed to those examples which, though less used, have been published and thoroughly canvassed; but less to those that have lain buried and forgotten in the closet or archives: for examples, like waters, are wholesomest in the running stream. 29. Precedents in law should not be derived from history, but from public acts and accurate traditions; for it is a certain infelicity, even among the best historians, that they dwell not sufficiently upon laws and judicial proceedings; or if they happen to have some regard thereto, yet their accounts are far from being authentic. 30. An

existing law determines the legal consciousness of the nation in no less degree than it originally was determined by it. Law therefore is also in terms of its content not merely the expression of general law-ideas and the national consciousness, but likewise the consequence of certain events of its establishment, and thus partly free personal act (by the legislator, leading jurists, merchants influential in legal affairs [Rechtsverkehr], landholders, etc.), partly accidental, often merely external influences and motives (ruling authorities, parties etc.). For this reason law can become alienated from the national consciousness in high degree, even to the point of contradicting it. But as long as it is not altered (in the manner set out by itself) the law asserts its full power and sanctity, this contradiction notwithstanding, for the sake of that independent existence.

§. 24. Law as Inheritance

Due to its subjective standpoint, the period of legal science and legal philosophy prior to the Historical School had no inkling that law arises in any other manner than through conscious human action, first through contractual, later through legislative establishment. People even thought that speech itself often came about through agreement! Custom, which despite all of this was encountered in life and in positive law, therefore was derived from the sanction of the legislator, even made into mediate legislation (Thibaut). Hugo was the first to emphasize the fact that custom is an independent source of law of no less importance than legislation. Savigny invested this fact, that law

---

example rejected in the same, or next succeeding age, should not easily be received again when the same case recurs; for it makes not so much in its favor that men sometimes used it, as in its disfavor that they dropped it upon experience. 31. Examples are things of direction and advice, not rules or orders, and therefore should be so managed as to bend the authority of former times to the service of the present. – RCA.]

springs from the popular consciousness through custom and later through scientific activity and thus develops in an organic manner, with its intellectual significance. This insight into the origin of law gained its juristic implementation through Puchta, to which Savigny added the finishing touches. In this manner a juristic science of the sources of law was gained which in its essential results appears to be assured for all future time. Moreover, Niebuhr and Savigny brought to awareness, in the teeth of the leading orientation of the times, the ethical principle of the venerableness of tradition and man's lot [Bescheidung] not to create an entirely new legal condition on his own strength. It is therefore a feature of piety, reverence for the higher constructive power over men, which characterizes the Historical School.

Certainly with this manner of doing things the danger arose of making the organic origin of law, which by all means recedes in later periods and only serves as a foundation, into the dominating and even the sole principle. This is the objection of *"naturalness"* [Naturwüchsigkeit]. In terms of principle this objection misses the mark, although the application of the new principle in its initial assertion may have gone overboard. This has been moderated for a long time now. Adjustment in this sense has always been praiseworthy and still is. Instead of this, however, opposition has arisen from the Hegelian school, which completely ignores this great and valuable significance of the Historical School and for its part puts forward an entirely opposed principle: the *absolutely free generation of the legal condition through the human spirit*. This principle, even though it is foreign to Hegel's own doctrine and in fact stands in opposition to it, is nevertheless the consistent result of a philosophy which elevates reason, coming to consciousness in men, into God. It is the principle of arrogance over against that of piety. The same spirit of allowing nothing validity but that which is produced by man freely by his cognition [Erkenntniß] likewise once filled Fichte. However, that which once was an innocent error acquires a different character when the truth has been brought to clear awareness. For the rest, this philosophical intention is not in any sense new. It is entirely the same conviction, in a rather more developed speculative form and duller edition [matterer Auflage], which was proclaimed by the Revolution of 1789 in simplicity and powerful action.[47]

---

[47]The latest polemic against the Historical School, from Beseler in his book *Popular Law and Learned Law*, is of an entirely different sort. The writer professes the viewpoint of the Historical School but characterizes its implementation until now as defective. The new doctrine of the sources of law which he opposes to it consists primarily in the assumption of a *popular law* distinguished in the same way from *customary* as from *learned law* and to be asserted over against both. This rests however on the same unacceptable presupposition as the previously commonplace concept of natural law, to wit, that a law exists which has not externally been fixed and implemented. Certainly a *popular consciousness* exists which is to be distinguished from custom, and which possibly no longer corresponds with custom, just as there exist law-ideas which are distinguished from positive laws. No one denies this. Then as to whether in Germany the existing law truly contradicts the popular consciousness and to what degree, and furthermore whether the reception of Roman law in its entirety and in specific areas took place through jurisprudence against the popular consciousness and popular need, are not principial but historical-factual questions regarding which therefore only individual opinions obtain, not the profession of a school of thought. However, a popular *law* alongside customary law can as little obtain as a law of reason alongside positive law. Popular consciousness which has not been fixed in custom – and it is the duration of observance which embodies the fixing – has no justification, no binding power, no capacity to be observed by the judge; and were the latter to attach such status to it, it would lead to

---

the inexpressible confusion and uncertainty of law. For the inner requirement (τέλος) of legal transactions and the intention of concerned parties
(merchants, landowners) in such transactions are certainly norms for the
judge, but that is not, and is not valid as, popular consciousness or popular
law, as little as natural law, but as the nature of the case (§. 10), which is not
disputed from any standpoint.

Chapter Four
The Popular Character of Law

§. 25. Law is the Product of Human Community, not Public Opinion

The law is to be the free human manifestation of God's order, thus at the same time the revelation [Offenbarung] of the human community's own ethically reasonable [sittlich verständigen] spirit and the subordination of its entire external condition to that order (§. 1). Accordingly, law arises from the consciousness of the people (§. 18), from its valuation of life, its innermost individuality (Savigny), and it arises in consonance with the entire condition of the people, the makeup of the land, climate, extent, means of subsistence, mores (Montesquieu); and precisely because of this, law arises in a living manner in the consciousness of the people, more or less generally known and understandable, or even, where such is not the case, at least generally recognized as that which is peculiar to it and indigenous. All of this taken together can be termed the *popular character* [Volksthümlichkeit] *of the law.* It is the condition in accordance with nature, it exists everywhere at the dawn of history, and there is great value in its being maintained.

By no means does it follow, however, that law must be in agreement with the prevailing opinion and legal point of view of the people. This firstly because the law above all must be in agreement with God's order, with reason and justice, to which even past customs and popular characteristics [Volksthümliche] must be subordinated. For example, in the case of the Romans and the Germans the pagan laws, even though

popular, had to give way to Christian ones. Popular character
has its worth as the special peculiar implementation of that
which is just and reasonable, not in what it is in itself, and especially not in opposition to the just and the reasonable. Furthermore, popular character is something entirely different
from the prevailing opinion of the people; it is the peculiarity
implanted in the people and growing during its entire history,
the effluence of its divine vocation, and the embodiment of the
actual, natural and spiritual requirements [Bedürfnisse] of its
particular condition. Prevailing opinion, on the other hand, is
opinion [Beurtheilung] adopted by the people possibly on the
basis of passion and error, which might even be an apostasy
from its own popular character, as in the case of the Jewish
people considering Baal and Moloch worship to be necessary
and advisable, or the same with the French people in 1789 regarding the republican form of government; there could be
nothing further from the popular character, in that Jewish popular customs and traditions [Volksthum] were based on
Jehovah-worship, French customs and traditions on the monarchy.

However, it most certainly follows that the maintenance
and restoration of indigenous laws over against a law received
from outside – the *nationality of the law* – and the general com-
prehensibility and accessibility of the law – the *popularity of the
law* – are an advantage and a goal. Still, the historical leading of
the peoples does not always allow of the attainment of this
goal everywhere and in full measure. Individual legal institutions of previously developed peoples, sometimes even their
entire legal edifice, press on and to that extent suppress original legal generation, leading in the developed situation of later
times to a technical development of the law which no longer
allows for ease of understanding and general legal expertise
[Rechtskunde]. The law itself, however, ever stands over the

popular character of law. This means that the justice and ap-
propriateness [Sachgemässheit] of norms, even continuity, as
that which in fact maintains the awareness of this justice and
necessity in the people (§. 15), form an even higher consideration than whether the law originated in this nation and
whether it now is generally understandable to, and known
among, this nation.

§. 26. The Gradual Detachment of Law from Popular Consciousness

Initially, national legal consciousness is itself naive and,
since mores and tradition predominate, it builds law in an immediate manner. There therefore exists a complete and immediate unity between it and the existing laws as its expression.
After reflection awakens, after legislation and science extend
their activity and external events [Ereignisse] step in with their
effects, this immediate unity must cease. The spiritual permeation of the law in the national consciousness must then become historical and systematic rather than naive, that is, the
legal norms are to be retained [festgehalten werden] as to their
causes [Veranlassungen], fortunes [Schicksalen], past applications, and explanations [Erörterungen], and in the coherence
of their effect [wirkung]. Such a permeation in its heightened
degree is ever a matter of special vital activity [Lebens-
thätigkeit], and therefore of a special class [Stand]. Not to allow
the gap which then arises between the general popular consciousness and the legal condition, or the scientific knowledge
[Erkenntniss] thereof, to become excessive, and to try to reduce it, is a worthy goal; the attempt to eliminate it, a vain one.
Codification in the misconceived version described above is an
example of the latter. Its intent is for the popular consciousness mechanically to reappropriate [wieder... aneignen] the

legal condition (that is, through external indoctrination or reference works from codes) which once was its own organically, i.e., as its own construction. In so doing it provides no true appropriation, while it endangers that historical and systematic permeation. One cannot give up scientific, historically developed theology in order to return to the simple undeveloped consciousness of God of the first Christian congregations, or wholly to replace it with the concept-less, bare theology of emotion of the current school. One cannot abandon scientific medicine based on anatomy, physiology, chemistry, in order to heal merely in accordance with mere doctor's discretion [ärztlichen Takt] or even with simple natural means. One cannot give up the technically developed art of war and allow the peoples to hit each other *en masse*. One cannot give up the comfort and mores of contemporary society in order to return to a simple state of nature. Just as well may one give up our legal science and legislation, which has gone far beyond the popular consciousness, in favor of a popular law. Simplicity, upon which general wisdom is founded, is always to be pursued, but never at the cost of truly proper [sachgemässen], fruitful [reichen] development.[48]

§. 27. Roman Law as Germany's Received Law

In the same manner every people initially had its self-constructed, purely national law. Events can occur, however, through which this law is irretrievably lost. Our German people was forced to accept the entire body of Roman law as formally valid [in förmlicher Geltung] for private law, as they have

---

[48]The now so widespread viewpoint that non-jurists could pass better judgement than jurists precisely because of their lack of knowledge which makes them impartial, is thereby similar to someone allowing laymen unprejudiced by medicinal systems to treat the sick, civilians to command armies.

in recent times had to accept English/French concepts, at least de facto, with regard to public law. Regarding the former the matter can certainly not be undone, regarding the latter virtually not. With respect to private law in particular, the complaint might be lodged that the reception of Roman law suppressed legal formation stemming from the peculiar spirit of the German nation in broader extension. What an advantage England had in this matter, where although it certainly underwent the influence of the learned Roman law, that law gained no formal validity, and the generation of law was effectuated entirely out of the peculiar national conviction. Even so, it cannot be denied that a higher leading was behind this. The Roman people had a mission from God to develop this aspect of human existence, the law, in an excellent manner and with an enduring truth, similar to the Greeks regarding art and the Jews regarding religion; and the appropriation of this its handiwork therefore cannot simply be termed an evil. Indeed, the Roman law is not owed an unconditional decisive regard, as little as is Greek art, but in the same way that the ancient world provides an indispensable foundation for the independent [selbständig] creative artist, so is the Roman law in certain degree the indispensable foundation of private law, not simply through its exemplary method but also through a range of apt decisions, through the disclosure of the nature of the case in relations of property law [Vermögensrechts].[49] Furthermore, a large portion of legal relations for which to us the Roman law is valid

---

[49]See the appendix to Book III of this volume. In this appendix (first in 1845) the question was first [überhaupt] examined which came up at the Germanist assembly of 1846. There on the one hand Roman law was recognized simply as an example of juristic method, on the other as a mixture of natural law and the nature of the case as written reason, from which the untenable result was derived that Roman law only "then is valid to the degree that it is justified by reason or has come into force in German form." Even so, voices testifying to the truth were not lacking.

had little connection with the national character, as for example purchase [Kauf], exchange [Tausch], tenancy [Miethe], eviction, etc., and the reverse is also true, Germanic law maintained and independently developed in broad degree those legal relations inseparably connected with the national valuation of life, as for example the entire law of persons, law of the family, rights of property within marriage [ehelichen Güterverhältnisse], relations based in landed property. All of this must therefore significantly moderate the complaint about the invasion of Roman law.

Be that as it may, the Roman law has become the law of Germany and has the power and regard derived from historical, centuries-long existence. Therefore it is never advisable to throw the Roman law overboard as a matter of principle, like something extraneous, in order thereby to restore the old Germanic law or entirely to make a newly to be created Germanic law tabula rasa. This would be a violation of the sanctity of law in itself; in fact it is a violation of nationality itself, in that the reverence for this law, with which the German imperial crown was bound up, is itself a deep-seated trait of German conviction and German history. As little as it is advisable, so little is it possible. The original generation of law by the German people cannot be set into motion again at the drop of a hat following three centuries of suppression. As something peculiarly Germanic and youthfully productive, this has not existed for a long while; there is therefore now neither a power of German legal generation available, nor can that now be retrieved which in the meantime would have proceeded from it had one preserved it from the Roman law. Against this, the historical putting down of roots by the Roman law is no hindrance to the truly advisable task of revitalizing German law, to the degree that vital power still resides in it; even to interpret it according to its own spirit and principle through science, praxis, legislation, rather than according to analogy of the Roman law; to get the Roman law to approach it through the historical pursuit and the proper understanding of its modifications in German practice, and in so doing – regardless of whether codes exist or not – to make ready a uniform legal consciousness through science.

§. 28. The False Understanding of the Popular Character of Law

The movement in favor of the popular character of law which manifested itself shortly before the catastrophe of 1848, and prior to that as symptom and precursor of that event, is based on entirely different principles from the ones laid down here in connection with Savigny and Montesquieu. Here for the first time the popular character of law – nationality and popularity – is considered to be the supreme, in fact the only viewpoint, against which the continuity of legal development, in fact justice itself, scarcely comes into view. Furthermore, the popular character of law is increasingly being invested with the meaning that law must answer to the current judgement and will of the people, and thus from now on must be determined by the people. In this manner indeed it is not so much the nationality and popularity of the law but much rather *popular sovereignty for the law*.

As means for this popular character, one therefore demands firstly the most extended codification *carried out by the popular assembly*, in order for the currently existing people to refound the entire legal condition. Accordingly, one demands *judges from the people* in twofold opposition, against the jurists [Rechtsgelehrten] and against the officials [Beamten], thus laymen elected by the people for a determinate periods of office: jurors [Geschworne] in criminal cases, lay assessors [Schöffen] in civil cases. These popular judges are not to be bound to the existing law but are themselves to make law, to be legislators in the individual case. In this manner lynch justice in particular is given a hitherto unheard-of significance. While jury members in terms of the English institution are bound in every respect by law, and in the French institution, while free from legal rules regarding evidence, are not free from legal characteristics regarding crime, and thus are only left to their personal (moral) conviction with regard to judgement of facts – in terms of this requirement of popular character jury members without exception will also pass judgement regarding the law in accordance with their personal conviction, thus e.g. not merely regarding whether the accused is guilty of high treason but whether high treason is punishable. The same thing will of necessity occur with the popular judge in the administration of civil justice. Actually, proponents have gone even further: the popular judge is not only not to be bound to existing law but not even to scientific rules, legal concepts and their consequences and coherence, but is to judge only according to his natural common sense (bons sens – cf. Kirchmann). Thus, legislation will continuously flow from the current sovereign people via their representative (to whom the king will not dare oppose a veto) and the administration of justice will yet be emancipated from this legislation under popular judges with sovereign power over the individual case. This will have the effect of the law complying with the contemporary opinion of the people, the latter finding no resistance in established laws and ordinances; but rather every one of its pulses immediately determining judicial decisions, as when e.g. the people, public opinion, no longer view high treason, lèse-majesté, adultery as crimes and therefore no longer punishable (even though still on the books as crimes), or when the people deems rental payments from peasants to be unjustified, and no judge recognizes them.

Beseler provided the initial impetus for this conception of the popular character of law, in that he was the first to depart from the proper conception of the Historical School.[50] For this runs in greater or lesser degree through the Germanist gatherings as a common characteristic.[51] In the final analysis, it

[50]Beseler, *loc. cit.* Beseler's viewpoint, unlike that of the subsequent movement, is not to furnish the objective structure of the law with its order, which although established and structured through history, practice, and science, is neither the product of the people, nor can it be fully understood by the people, nor does it any longer correspond to its will; but only to foster the newly generating powers of the present, scientifically to investigate the continually new forms of national commerce (e.g., among landowners, merchants); in this, his national tendency is justified. However, he first posits the principle of the legal validity of the popular consciousness, and substitutes a law of determinative popular consciousness, the principle of this movement, for the popular consciousness bound to the law, which is the principle of the Historical School, and he partly forges the means which the subsequent movement is pushing to the limit.

[51]At the Germanists' assemblies at Frankfurt and Lübeck in 1846 and 1847, the well-grounded and timely pursuit of German nationality and thus of the nurture of Germanic law was permeated and, I might add, thwarted by this false notion of popular character. Regardless of the moderations and protestations of estimable voices, the leading element of these convocations nevertheless was the lack of recognition for the continuity of law and its many hundreds of years of existence – the desire for a radical elimination of Roman law, either immediate or gradual – the imperceptible substitution by which the concept of Germanic law is transformed into the legal judgement of the learned, the capacities of which one became convinced in the chambers of Baden etc. – the demand for universal codification – the conception of the institution of the jury as the voice of the people, which with regard to the laws discovers the justice and actual guilt of individual cases, replaces the princes' right of pardon, purifies of unjust laws – the argument against Roman law, that the laity cannot become versed in it, that their right depends on whether the judge has studied in Berlin or Heidelberg, as if one might not, through a good handbook, become just as well versed in the common law as in a new code, which itself is not lacking in amendments and determinations from practice, and as if a modern constitutional or civil law code does not have its controversies just as well as Roman law does – an argument which besides is much more valid against German private law and therefore demonstrates that it is not so much the national as it is the modern form of legal condition (codification according to the current popular viewpoint) which this movement is targeting.

is men of secondary importance who have fully developed it and carried it out to its most extreme expression.[52] But even now in popular opinion, in many cases there is a lack of clarity and the confusion of the popular character of law, which is natural and an advantage, with the popular sovereignty of the law, which is overthrow and destruction.

This movement in pursuit of popular character advanced together with a polemic against Roman law, in a certain connection with Germanistic efforts. Although by many these efforts were meant seriously, the strength of the current at that time went against the Roman law not simply because it was Roman but because it was a historically developed law binding the present and binding the current popular will. And it aimed for Germanic law as little as it did Roman; rather, it merely aimed for the will of the contemporary German people. The people, to whom one wishes to hand a codification, from whom one wishes a sovereign judge to arise, will never produce Germanic law but a law in accordance with contemporary political science, precisely as good as and in fact much closer to the doctrine of the Romance [romanischen] peoples. Experience has demonstrated this. At the German national assembly in Frankfurt in 1848, where the proponents – moreover, the moderate proponents – of this viewpoint exercised decisive influence, everything (after in 1846 having proclaimed that "in the great act of founding a German collective legislation only German law can be laid at the foundation") that remained of actual Germanic law was eliminated root and branch: family estates [Stammgüter], estates in fee [Lehngüter], rights of rank [Standesrechte], corporations founded in hierarchy [Abstufung]

---

[52]E.g. Kirchmann, *The Uselessness of Jurisprudence as a Science* (see thereagainst my article, "Legal Science or Popular Consciousness?"). Eberti, *Journal*. Leue, *German Lay Tribunals* (a writing which received the approval of Mittermaier in Lübeck).

and superiority; and in their place pure Romanistic institutions were proclaimed as German fundamental rights: Roman simple property, French-style corporations based simply upon the number of votes [Stimmenzahl], etc. This undeniably testifies to a democratic rather than a Germanistic tendency.

This trend confronted the Historical School in pronounced animosity, even though the latter was the first to bring to awareness the coherence between the law and the consciousness and peculiarity of the people, and even though from it and only from it did the actual revival of Germanic elements of our legal condition stem, and only through its method can they actually be furthered. There is however this distinction: the Historical School bases the law on the people in its collective history, while the popular-character movement bases it on the contemporaneous people. In the former case, the law is based upon the people in terms of its full extent and articulated relations, in which the ruling authority and jurists are an essential and specially appointed [berufene] part of it; in the latter, upon the people in the modern democratic sense, in opposition to ruling authority and jurists. In the former, the people are to generate law in order to obey specific norms as being bound to them – in custom and tradition; in the latter, in order to command the norms that it considers good.

In its complete development [Ausbildung] (and the more so, the more it approaches this) the popular character of law as hereby pursued is an emancipation from everything toward which a constraint [Gebundenheit] should exist: emancipation of the present from the past, emancipation of subjects from the orders [Anordnungen] of ruling authority, emancipation of the subjects from the legislative power, emancipation of human judgement from the laws of the matter [Gesetzen der Sache] as presented by science. It is a confirmation of the democratic principle that it establish itself in the area of the administration of justice as well as that of the constitution. Because when in this manner penal authority simply is opened up to the people as it sees fit, no ruling authority can stand against the will of the people. It is however in the end the *destruction of the administration of justice:* through it, that which it is the primary, in fact sole, business of the administration of justice, justice itself, is banished from it. Justice means that the judicial verdict be declared simply according to immutable laws, in accordance with merit and guilt; a historically developed, evenhandedly administered law provides a guarantee of this, with its clearly determined norms and learned corps of judges [Richterstand], for whom at least, even though everywhere subject to that which is human, it is the spirit and honor of the profession [Standesgeist... Standesehre] to subordinate all personal inclinations and disinclinations to the laws. Against this, such popular judges render decisions, as the nature of the case and as experience everywhere confirms, in accordance with emotion and passion, be it according to hate and jealousy, partiality of class [Stände], or according to prevailing currents of political opinion or party, or according to sentimentality. And justice no less means that the verdicts in the entire country for all similar [gleichbeschaffenen] cases be in agreement with each other, the entire administration of justice be ordered by one and the same (ethical) order of life [Lebensordnung], all cases be determined as if by one act, all men weighed with an equal balance, and this safeguard is also achieved by a historically developed law and an educated corps of jurists [gelehrter Richterstand]. Against this, popular judges are informed only by their own conviction, and under exactly the same conditions render one decision in one case, a different decision in another; their decisions are unpredictable, for one and the same act here passing down a death sentence, there acquittal and praise; under equal conditions the contracting party, the pensioner [Rentenberechtigte], hereditary tenant [Erbverpächter] here triumph, there are defeated. The entire administration of justice hereby becomes a chaos of individual, mutually conflicting decisions.

Chapter Five
Legal Obligation

§. 29. The Twofold Nature of Legal Obligation

The obligation applied by the existing (positive) law is *legal obligation.* Accordingly it comprehends both the obligation of individuals to obey the law and the obligation of the community, i.e. the ruling authority, to maintain the law. The obligation first to restore the law according to its true ideas is, by contrast, a moral duty of the community and its power-holders.

§. 30. Legal versus Moral Obligation

In line with the nature of law, the character of legal obligation is that of *external duty*, i.e., that it proceed to men from external (objective) existence; and it has this external existence as its aim. From this are derived the individual characteristics which distinguish legal from moral obligation:[53]

I. Legal obligation is concerned *merely with the action,* not, as is the case with moral obligation, with the *motive.* This is because the latter is not necessary to maintain the external order – Kant's distinction between *legality* and *morality.*

---

[53]The earlier natural law made its primary task the elucidation of this distinction. Since the speculative legal philosophy, one considers himself absolved of this. But that general construction – leaving aside its intrinsic value – in no way justifies the abandonment of the implementation of keen determinations of judgement.

2.   Legal obligation is only *negative*,[54] for its goal is already fulfilled: it is the already realized external order of common life. The requirement of legal obligation is simply not to interrupt that order in its regular operation. When for example a debt is paid, a police order is performed, nothing new occurs, only routine existence is not interrupted. By contrast, the aim of moral obligation, the inward completion of men and their devotion to persons and ideas is a matter of a continuously creative positive act. The fulfillment of ethical obligation therefore is capable of infinite elevation; legal obligation, on the other hand, is either fulfilled or it is not. From this as well comes the nomenclature: "law" [Recht – lit. "straight" – RCA] the negative, what cannot be omitted, in opposition to "good," the positive good.

3.   Precisely for this reason, ethical obligation in each specific case first obtains its individualization through the individual and his freedom, and therefore *is not recognizable* ahead of time with regard to that case ("in concreto"). Legal obligation, on the other hand, already gains its individualization through the common will (this is precisely positive law) and therefore is exactly and completely indicated [vorgezeichnet] and recognizable for each specific case ("in concreto"). So for example it is determinable in concreto that the debtor must pay, and how much; but regarding sharing from a motivation of love, the form, measure, person of the

---

[54]This is something other than the *content* of law in our given condition being of a mere negative character, regarding which see above, ch. 1.

recipient are indeterminate.

4. Finally, legal obligation must be *unfailingly fulfilled.* As objective order, it cannot depend on either the judgement of the individual regarding his duty in a specific case (consideration of conscience [Gewissensüberlegung]) or from his considerations to obey. It is therefore *coercible*, which is to say, coercible *via legal action* [von Rechtswegen], so that the one coerced is aware of yielding not to a physical power but physically to an ethical power. The inward perfection of men excludes coercion; the uninterrupted continuance of external order requires it.[55] Even with legal obligation, however, coercion remains in the background. Law is not a natural order, from the outset realizing itself through physical force; it ever remains an ethical order, an order for human action, and since, in terms of the true structure of the human race, that order is always freely fulfilled, so it is also in our given condition meant freely to be fulfilled, and coercion only arises when men resist. Because law is an ethical order, it is *freely to be* fulfilled; but because it is an *objective* order, it *must* be fulfilled. In normal circumstances this coercion is exercised by the *ruling authority.* However, where such does not exist, prior to or outside of the state relation [Staatsverbandes], the requirement of uninterrupted continuance expresses itself in the authorization of *self-help* and the obligation upon all *others to provide aid.*

---

[55]Accordingly, coercion is not derived from the requirement of individual freedom (Kant, Fichte) but from the requirement of the uninterrupted order of common life.

§. 31. Legal Obligation versus Coercibility

In line with this, however, coercibility is only the consequence, not the primary characteristic of legal obligation. The
latter consists much rather in the commonality (objectivity) of
the norm and thus in the requirement of unfailing fulfillment
independently of all subjective considerations of conscience.
For this reason coercibility and especially [vollends] ordered,
fully guaranteed coercibility is by no means a decisive criterion
for legal obligation. On the contrary, there are exceptions in
which legal obligation cannot be coerced – when either the real
power punishing those who are refractory or the higher authority representing the legal order fails to exercise
coercion – without it thereby ceasing to be legal obligation, and
coming to coincide with moral obligation. These exceptions
are primarily two:

1. *The duties of the law of nations,* for example to keep
   treaties, to respect the extraterritoriality of ambas-
   sadors, which obviously have an entirely different
   character than the duties of the *morals of nations*
   [Völkermoral], for instance to come to the aid of
   an oppressed people, not to interrupt the trade of
   another nation; they are the common norms, recognized as inviolable and unfailingly to be fulfilled;
   for this reason the law of nations is unjustifiably
   denied a juridical character.

2. *The duties of princes to the laws of the state,* namely *the
   national constitution.* These are essentially different
   from the *ethical* duties of regents. The latter depend
   on their moral judgement in each individual case,
   in which they are to decide merely in accordance

with their conscience; the former, by contrast, are an unconditional requirement, independent of examination by conscience, which are simply to be fulfilled if princes are not to act in a manner contrary to law, and thus unconditionally unethically.[56] It is therefore erroneous to consider these duties to be coercible in the way that the French Revolution declared them;[57] but just because they are not coercible it is no less erroneous to consider them to be mere moral duties in the manner in which the Hallerian school, at least in part, considers them. The former abolishes all authority and thus the legal order itself; the latter places the entire legal existence of common life in the conscience of the prince, so that he vouchsafes it in the same way as almsgiving, and therefore is the true absolutism.

The distinction between uncoercible legal obligations and moral obligations is by no means hairsplitting. Legal obligation always has external effect even when not the final one of coercibility and its guaranteed result. The violation of the duties of the law of nations grounds the *lawful war* (casus belli), and thus coercion by legal action, albeit accompanied by factual uncertainty; and the violation of the nation's constitution and the laws of the land by the prince entitles subjects to *protestation* [Protestation] and *passive resistance*, while nonfulfillment of moral duties of regents only lead to remonstrations [Remon-

---

[56]So for example a prince, even though with the strongest conviction of conscience that the new constitutions are no good, may not abolish such a constitution existing in his country.

[57]1793. *Declaration of Rights* Art. 35: "Should the government infringe the rights of the people, the insurrection of the people and every individual part of the people is the holiest of its rights and highest of its duties." Lafayette has lately spoken publically in this manner.

strationen].[58]

---

[58]Accordingly, the duty of Protestant territorial princes only to exercise their ecclesiastical power according to the counsel of the clergy belongs to the legal (constitutional) duties, even if not enforceable. Omission justifies not merely remonstration but protestation. Richter's statement (*Textbook of Ecclesiastical Law*, §. 50) that the prince has "the *ethical* obligation to be advised by theologians" rests on an improper concept of legal and moral duty. Even so, in that he includes this apparently only moral duty in his book on ecclesiastical law, Richter gives unwitting testimony that it must after all have a juridical character.

Chapter Six
Law in the Subjective Sense or Rights

§. 32. Subjective Right as the Power of the Individual

The law as the objective-ethical form of life both gives specific form to human life relations and allots, and ethically protects, the spheres of the existence and action of men and satisfaction in those spheres (§.1., §. 4.). But by virtue of the personality of men, the essence of which is self-causation and concentration (relation back [Rückbeziehung]) upon himself, the sphere which is allotted to him through the ethical power of law is of necessity *his own ethical power inhering in himself over against others*, who then are ethically bound *to him* – not merely to God or their conscience or the legal order with respect to him – he is not merely an *object* of their duty but the *cause* of it. This is law *in the subjective sense* or *rights*.[59]

Accordingly, law in the subjective sense is the *ethical power* which a man has over against others in the sphere allotted to him by the legal order, by virtue of that order. Its essence is not merely the negative of allowance or the intransitive [lacking a direct object – RCA] of freedom, but the positive and transitive [having a direct object – RCA] of ethical power against others. Allowance and freedom are not always but only frequently the same with regard to content. In particular, neither does freedom coincide with law in the subjective sense. It is partly more extended, while man has natural freedom from God which as such is not yet entitlement,[60] and partly more re

---

[59]Rights thus construct the existence of people in the ethical world, which is their own ethical power, in the same way that their existence in the physical world is their own physical power.

[60]Here belong the use of our corporeal organs, e.g., "the nose to

stricted, while there are rights which freedom does not under-
lie, as for example life. Neither does law in the subjective sense
come to the same thing as will, but much rather to the power a
will (better, a personality) has over other wills.

By its concept, law in the subjective sense can only be
attributed to a personality, and only by virtue of a higher order.
We therefore do not attribute rights to legal institutions as such
(e.g., marriage), since they are not personalities, though it be
that they are treated in that manner through artificial transfer-
ence; and we attribute no rights to God, because He does not
have ethical power over us by virtue of a higher order – He
Himself is that ethical power.[61]

Law in the subjective sense, e.g., the right of men due
him in all his life positions, constructs, in that it is his own
power inhering in him, a true center about which the entire
external world (things, actions of others, etc.) is related as con-
trolled object, and in accordance with which the content of
legal norms is often determined. It is therefore a *secondary principle of the legal order* alongside the primary and absolute principle:
the *purpose* (τέλος) of *life relations*. As secondary principle, however, it is always based upon this latter. Its own content and

---

smell," the freedom to sleep or to awake and the like. To conceptualize as a
right anything which does not refer to other people, thus to the ethical
world, leads to the absurdity which confronts us in the question regarding
the "right to smell." Cf. Book III. §. 2.

[61]To speak of a right of the world-spirit, as Hegel does, is therefore
from his own standpoint entirely inappropriate. Likewise one cannot really
speak of a right (e.g., entitlement) of marriage, of the family, to wit, in a
manner similar to Schelling when he says: "all desire is will, will is that
which puts up resistance in matter": in this manner one might say that all
existence in the ethical world is law (in the subjective sense), this is what
offers resistance to the one who is transgressing. Even so, it would be improper. As little as we may ascribe will in the actual sense to matter, as little
may we ascribe rights to institutions as such. In matter it is a higher will that
has placed the physical power of resistance in matter; in the ethical world it
is the same higher will that has placed its ethical power in this institution. It
is not its own power, as in the case of the personality of people.

range is originally and essentially derived from, and the coherence of all the rights of all men lies in, this objective higher principle.

§. 33. Rights are Independent of Duties

Rights arise from God's world order and belong to it in the same way that the ethical form of life relations does, thus no less than does the existence and power of personalities. Hence, our rights are not the consequence of the duty of others; much rather, that duty is the consequence of our rights in the specific case. They are not the consequence of our own duty but the original immediate content of the legal order. Certainly rights are preconditions of dutiful action; devotion is not possible apart from existence and power. But they are in no way mere means to that end;[62] rather they are due one simply because of his personality. They are an original independent purpose no less than is fulfillment of one's duty. For God desires the existence of personalities – and the rights attendant to them – as an end in itself to the same degree that He desires their duty-inspired decision as an end in itself. Rights therefore are *imparted to man with the first breath through which the divine essence is imparted to him.* Even so, our rights stand in coherence with

---

[62]According to Kant, man only has external freedom (entitlement) with a view to morality, that is, he has it in order that reason (the logical law of universality together with the law of non-contradiction) has absolute causality in the world; he does not vindicate this causality for human personality *as such*. It is therefore according to his own standpoint consistent but improper when Kant deduces the right of personality in terms of duty (*Doctrine of Law* [Rechtslehre], XLIII): "do not allow yourself to be used as a means." This duty to safeguard my independence is something entirely other than the right of personality, i.e., the ethical power over others, in order that they *may* not use me as a means. With regard to the insoluble difficulties encountered by the old natural law in deducing the concept of right in the subjective sense, see Vol. I, Book III, §. 2, ch. 2.

our duties. For it is one and the same world plan from which
both spring and in which they are related to each other in
unity. The higher uniting factor which embraces duties and
rights is *vocation* (§. 5). Duties arise from vocation, as do rights,
and vocation is the standard against which both are measured.
It is the *ethical, specifically Christian conception to consider rights only in
the light of vocation.* Certainly, in the condition of perfection
men's rights and their ethical will always differ somewhat, each
is arch-independent, albeit without contradicting the other: the
entitled will seeks none other than that which is ethical. But
although man no longer answers to his true ethical nature, nevertheless his personality and therefore also his entitlement by
no means is extinguished for that reason, precisely because this
is an independent goal that does not coincide with morality.
The human will yet exercises power over others even where it
itself has ceased to will that which is ethical. Rights therefore
are to be considered holy by men even where they are abused
for countermoral [moralwidrigen] (egotistical) goals. This
therefore answers to that divine purpose wherein that which is
innermost in men, whether good or evil, is to manifest itself
decisively here below (Matthew 13:29).

§. 34. The Relationship between Rights and Duties

And so rights are not derived first from duty but from
the immediate original content of law. Nevertheless, they do
not form *the* content of law pure and simple, that is, its sole
and "actual" content, in which case legal duties are not original
but derived from rights; but they belong together with them to
the content of law. For the law does not merely impart to men
their determinate existence and position in the ethical world; it
above all gives shape to the ethical world itself, and therefore
consists just as much in commands for the maintenance of the

proper form of institutions as in commands for the security of human positions. The content of the former commands therefore is mere duties or necessities, not however rights, e.g., the prohibition on incest, polygamy, divorce out of mutual agreement, the command to punish crime, and the like.[63]

Therefore, although a duty must correspond to each right as its effect, in no way must the reverse be true, that every right (or every necessity) correspond to a duty as its cause.

In a higher sense, certainly that which is an ethical law of life relations, which is God's order over men, at the same time is also a right of man itself by virtue of the unity of its innermost essence with this order. So for example spouses who divorce by mutual agreement or who live in incestuous marriage not only violate God's order but at the same time also the right of others and their own right; blasphemy is not merely sacrilege against God but at the same time also an affront to the one who confesses God, to the believing congregation. It is even the right of the murderer to be put to death. Nevertheless, it is not the bare entitlement of the human will, by which

---

[63]Therefore when Puchta bases his system on the contention that "the *actual* content of law is rights" (preface to *Pandects*, I, 6th edition), for this reason alone (apart from the untenability of making the category of objects the basis for division) it must be rejected by us. It cannot be in the manner of rights of the community that one maintains the prohibition on incest, the punishment of crime, etc. The community does not maintain this as its right but as an order over it which is transferred to it for safekeeping. I have not denied that law includes rights in its essential content; therefore the citation from Genesis 1:26 was unnecessary in this context. On the contrary, I asserted, contrary to my previous conception, that rights form an immediate content and independent purpose of law by virtue of the personality of men, and not in consequence of duties or as means for duties, that they "are imparted to men with the first breath imparted to him by the divine Being" (p. 130 of the 1st edition). Thereagainst, I am unable to recognize that "rights form the *actual* content of law" and thus that those higher ordinances and requirements are only an *improper* content of law. Apart from this, Puchta (*Institutes*, 1841) described the significance of right in the subjective sense in its full intensity.

it manifests itself as determinative principle, as prime cause and final goal; it is entitlement by virtue of the pervasiveness [Erfülltheit] of the ethical world order; and therefore that order is perceived as their right only by the ethically deepest and purest men, while it seems by the general and initial view simply to be a limitation of their right.

Those duties which correspond to the rights of others are therefore something entirely specific, something other than legal obligation in general as distinct from moral duty (§. 29). Legal obligation in general is that which is laid upon us by the legal order as distinguished from morality even when it does not stem from the entitlement of another; for example, the prohibition on incest, the duty on the part of subjects to serve in the armed forces [Kriegspflicht des Unterthanen]. With this specific class of duties, however, there is the peculiarity of having the right of another as ground and center. One must consider all duties which lack their origin in such an entitlement to be the logical opposite of this class. In particular, though, the *duties of love* form an opposite to these duties, because while these are the consequence of the ethical existence and power of others and consist in their not being violated, duties of love are the preservation, usually through self-sacrifice, of that which does not yet belong to the ethical existence and power of others, at disadvantage to one's own existence. Not to murder one's neighbor, not to snatch his captured wildlife, is a duty arising from his existing right. By contrast, to come to the aid of one's neighbor against rapacious animals, to protect him or to help him kill them, is not the consequence of existence in the ethical world as guaranteed him by God, but an expansion and enrichment of his existence through his own devotion. The duties of love do not however exhaust all moral duties and do not exhaust all original duties not derived from any entitlement, but only form the material opposite to that other relation in which allocated, secured existence is not violated.

§. 35. Public Rights

The primary sphere of rights is private law, since it has the individual person as its goal. However, the position or power assumed by a person in his relation to public law becomes his right by virtue of his personality and in accordance with his nature. There are therefore public entitlements as well, that is, those which exist in public relations and for public goals (§. 48.). Entitlement as such is however always a person's. In terms of competence [Zuständigkeit], of the relation to the subject, it is private, since a right or entitlement is in fact an attribute [Attribution] of the individual. Only the relation in which, and the final goal for which, the entitlement exists makes it into a public one, for the content and manner of use is determined accordingly.[64]

§. 36. Innate versus Acquired Rights

Rights are due a person either simply for the benefit of, and with, his existence as personality, or for specific conditions and therefore in consequence of specific characteristics, actions and circumstances. The former are termed *"innate,"* the latter *"acquired"* rights; perhaps more appropriately, *general* and *specific* rights. To the former belong life, liberty, honor, afterwards the general capacity for property, family, political and ecclesiastical rights; to the latter belongs every actually existing right issuing from that general capacity.[65]

---

[64]This finds its application namely regarding the question as to whether the royal power is public or private.

[65]The literal concept of innate and acquired does not adequately describe the distinction here intended; for e.g. the nobility or the sonship in

An entirely different opposition as this is that of the *pri-meval right* [Urrecht] of men versus *actual rights*, that is, the rights (and in fact both sorts, the general as well as the particular) as they *ought* to be due to men in line with the idea of man, versus rights as they actually *are* due him in the given situation. German natural law theory intermingled both oppositions, putting primeval right and innate rights on a line, and setting particular rights, instead of the existing inadequate legal condition, in opposition to the primeval right. Against this, the French Revolution's theory of the rights of men holds fast to the latter opposition with clear awareness, but it conceives it falsely. That is to say, it understands by "the rights of men" those which are to be derived from the concept of man as *valid a priori* and which therefore supposedly have no need of positive law, which cannot *lawfully* and in a *legally* binding manner be deprived or restricted. Their opposite thus becomes the positive-legal rights, which then however have no validity in conflict with these and which in fact, it was desired, should be eliminated altogether.

However, *in the first place* this concept of the primeval right, or the rights of men so conceived, that is, which have the effect it ascribes to them, is worthless. There exists just as little an opposition and a dividing line between primeval right and the rights of positive law as between the law of reason and positive law. In terms of his idea (thus by nature), man of necessity has rights just as the community has a legal order, but which rights he has is everywhere first more specifically determined by positive law.[66] The latter can be unjust in this, but

a family do not form part of innate rights in this sense. I summarize so-called innate rights as the right of personality and therefore treat them as such below in private law.

[66]For this reason the concept of "*natural* coercive law" put forward by most natural-law proponents is as untenable as is the concept of "*natural law.*"

lawfulness can be decided only on its terms. The claims of serfs and peasants [Grundholden] deduced therefrom for the emancipation of their persons and possessions, or those of burghers to equal political position to the nobility, or those of the people to participate in sovereignty, were, leaving aside the question of truth or untruth, in none of those cases *actual rights*, i.e., already valid, made effective by coercion, over against which existing rights could be considered unlawful.

In the second place, that concept of primeval right or the rights of men is not the true primeval right in terms of content. On the one hand, the rights which it is to include, such as e.g. equal participation in state power and the like, are themselves in terms of the law-idea not claims that can be realized every-where and unconditionally in the way that for instance the abo-lition of serfdom in truth is such a claim. On the other hand, they are insufficient to exhaust the right which is due men by virtue of his idea. For in the case of political rights which make up the content of the "rights of men," which moreover only concern formal equality, the individual citizen might die of hunger, as chides the Communist doctrine, or become stifled [verdumpfen] in barbarism.[67] The *true primeval right* due to men as personality is not simply the fullest freedom and political entitlement but also the fullest *satisfaction* and *highest spiritual perfection*. The primeval right therefore cannot be realized but is only amenable to steady approximation. Civil society is to strive to realize the idea of primeval right, but it cannot "claim

---

[67]The German natural-law theory, certainly of the primeval right of men, is of course even more threadbare than the French rights of man; because in consequence of that confusion it only includes the rights de-scribed above as "innate," these mere possibilities, as its content, and in fact arrives at the conclusion that the primeval right only consists in negatives, in being "non-means," "non-things" (see Vol. I, 2nd edition, pp. 138-139), or in the abstract capacity to be able contractually to obligate anyone else to the same thing to which one may obligate him (Kant).

it back" [wieder fordern], since it was never in its possession.

On this depends the erstwhile oft-discussed question regarding the *inalienability of rights.* Properly understood, the inalienability of rights, just as the disposability of rights in general, focuses on whether rights are due a person for a position ethically necessary to him or merely for his satisfaction or his freedom. Accordingly, not only innate rights (life, freedom etc.) but also many acquired (particular) rights, e.g. the right of marriage, paternal power, are not disposable and not alienable. Such rights ever remain just as much duties as well. To use the ancient expression, they may be a potentia activa since in accordance with the above every right is a power inhering in man himself, prohibiting violation by another, but they are not, at least not in every respect, a facultas. This is the true and simple principle regarding the alienability of rights. But in that discussion one understands by alienability and inalienability the question whether men (i.e., the great majority) may in terms of legal obligation lack certain rights (to wit, the right to govern, to make laws), which one views, under the false supposition that the civil order rests on contract, as an alienation of that condition,[68] and accordingly one wishes to decide whether they belong to the primeval right of men in that sense. The untenableness of the question itself as well as that of the standard of judgement is clear from the above. The thus corrected question as to the degree of restricted legal capacity [Rechtsfähigkeit] allowable in terms of the law-ideas will be dealt with in the section below[69] concerning the right of personality.

§. 37. The Origin and Cessation of Rights

---

[68]Thus Fichte in his anonymous writing: *Contribution to the Rectification of the Public's Verdict Regarding the French Revolution.*

[69]Book III, *Private Law*, §. 2ff.

The grounds of the origin and cessation of rights are infinitely manifold each in accordance with the content and sphere of life in which they intervene.[70] Nevertheless, in general they may be classified under two main headings in accordance with the two principles of the legal order: the purpose of life relations, and human entitlement and freedom. Accordingly, rights arise either:

1. through *will* and *act*, be it one's own, be it another's, be it both at the same time (e.g. occupation, testament, contract, tort, royal grant, popular election and the like); or,

2. *of their own accord, through given processes and relations* (accession, versio in rem, lineage, kindredship, and the like), in particular as the consequence and result of a more comprehensive – originating either voluntarily or involuntarily – legal relation (e.g. the right to alimony by filiation and the like). In the first case, rights arise by means of human freedom; in the second, "directly through the law" (lege).[71]

§. 38. The Doctrine of Prescription

Finally, another general ground of the origin and cessation of rights is *prescription* [Verjährung]. This is deeply rooted

---

[70]It is self-evident that property, obligation, inheritance, trade privilege, nobility, royal power, civil office, ecclesiastical office, easements, etc., do not originate and are not extinguished through the same or similar grounds

[71]Only in this sense is it proper when partly the Romans and partly the moderns talk of *legal* [gesetzlichem] rights of pledge, *legal* inheritance, *legal* claims as a separate class; for in the final analysis the other classes must also be grounded in the law. The more appropriate distinction is: the action of the participants, and the relation inherent in the thing.

in the essence of the law; for law has the twofold root of its existence in the general consciousness and in establishment in outward life. Time however, and time in its further exercise (positive or negative) manifests [äussern] a power on both, on the consciousness and habituation [Gewöhnung] of men as well as on establishment in outward conditions, the latter through entanglement with infinitely many lawful relations and infinitely many reasonable transactions already erected upon this practice [Ausübung]. The condition of prescription [verjährte Bestand] thusly is transformed into a legally conse-crated one, entirely analogously to the manner in which cus-tomary law develops.[72] Now then, an expression of this inward necessary power of time and practice is the confusion which arises in case one does not recognize it. This principle of pre-scription therefore has its effect in many areas of law, for ex-ample the adverse possession [Ersitzung] of property, real rights, regalia, the statute of limitations regarding accusation, the (German-legal) acquisition of a higher rank through exer-cise into the third generation, the (factually valid) eventual le-gitimation of a usurped throne, and even the statute of limita-tions on punishment.

The duration of prescription must of necessity vary ac-cording to the nature of the right in question. Regarding rights of a public character, it is usually in accordance with nature the time of general human memory (quod memoriam excedit) or more precisely stated, the length of three generations.[73]

---

[72]It is self-evident that this parallel is not meant to contradict the distinction made by Puchta between customary law and prescription, with its practical consequences for the demonstration of the former. Prescription has a ground and significance for law in the subjective sense similar to what custom has for law in the objective sense. To the degree that law in the subjective and in the objective sense are to be kept apart, to no less degree are prescription and custom to be so.

[73]See Savigny, *System*, IV. 481ff., and Homeyer, *Saxon Mirror*, II. 2., pp. 305 and 643.

In terms of the standpoint of the older school of natural law, no origin of rights can be conceived apart from the free will of the acquirer and of the one obligating himself. Prescription is therefore viewed as a means of acquisition not by natural law but only by positive law. Indeed, however, from that viewpoint neither can the in rem versio, the obligation from the negotiorum gestio, the condictio sine causa, in fact even intestate succession and the like be recognized as truly lawful. The objection to the "natural law" validity of prescription, that reason cannot give the degree [Maaß] thereof, rests on the false assumption that the other legal institutions have a precise and determinate form already by virtue of their law-ideas. The other objection, that one's right cannot expire apart from his will, would, if it were correct, affix the label of injustice on the positive institution of prescription; but it is incorrect because rights resting on the will of the entitled continuously require, in accordance with their nature, an up-to-dateness [ein Aktualität] of that will. Now then, even though – in line with the limitations of human nature – an uninterrupted awareness and assertion of rights cannot be required, still the complete lack of up-to-dateness has a limit beyond which it must lead to the loss thereof.

Chapter Seven
The System of Law

§. 39. Legal Relations and Institutions

If law is the order of human common life, then the system of law is the coherency of *life relations in their legal order*, i.e., a coherency of *legal relations* and *legal institutions*.

These are complexes of facts and factual relations and their legal norms, which together, through the unity of the *purpose* (τέλος) *inhering in them*, form an indissoluble whole.[74] To wit, I understand by legal relation the life relations which have the purpose of being a part of the legal order (e.g. property, marriage, inheritance)[75]; by legal institution, the same relations to the degree that they already attained their legal ordering. Each legal institution is accordingly in turn itself an order, and the law, it being the total order of human common life, thus in turn unfolds itself in orders, i.e., in just those legal institutions.

§. 40. Factual and Legal Relations

The coherence of law, as ethical power, with life relations is however a coherence in which law takes hold of these

---

[74]For example, the pledge relation *and the law of pledge* arises from the purpose of vouchsafing security to the creditor by means of objects of property. From this spring the law of pledge's manifold concepts in their entirety – the dependent nature, the restriction of rights to mere alienation, the real action [dingliche Klage (i.e., actio in rem – RCA)], the distinction between movable and immovable collateral, the consideration of priority, etc.

[75]Therefore I cannot for myself accept the example used by Savigny of lex frater a fratre. This law contains a legal *case*, not a legal *relation* in this technical sense.

relations as its factual [faktischen] material and sets them into an ethical form. The law as ethical constructive power thus advances in life relations as factual material; this, then, is the course the system takes [und das ist denn auch den Gang des Systems]. But the same purpose (τέλος) which is effectuated by the legal arrangement is also already active in the bare factual relations (§. 5) and vice versa, the legal order for its part creates a multitude of factual relations. For this reason the factual and the legal (life relations and legal institutions) are distinguishable but not separable, and the system, conceived as total effect, advances in legal institutions, although these institutions have natural life relations as their presupposition, as their a priori. This is the successiveness [Aufeinanderfolge] of legal institutions, or of life relations to the degree that they maintain their legal content.

§. 41. The Ongoing Development of Legal Institutions

The sequence of legal institutions, first the life relations and then the already legally active institutions, therefore rests upon their actually (realiter) preceding and following each other as conditioning and conditioned. Whether logically they are simple or complex is not decisive. So for example, private law naturally precedes public law, personality precedes property, marriage precedes paternal power, family law precedes the law of inheritance. Only that with everything organic a member is not a mere precondition of the other but ever and again is conditioned by the other, at least if it is to fulfill its purpose; so, for example, the state already appears as determinative and form-giving for private law as well. Furthermore, legal relations are always jointly generating new such relations: so for example the law of inheritance springs from the purpose of property and the family together, the law of pledge from the law of things and of obligations together. Such institutions therefore depend on a double root.

§. 42. The Enduring Character of the Legal System

Just as the content of law changes, so of necessity does its coherency. The legal construction of each people, and of each epoch thereof, therefore has its own system. But the character of the legal system, which is that of a coherency of legal institutions, remains always. In the same way, it is also from these same fundamental relations that the legal condition of all, at least all civilized, peoples equally must exist; only that with each it is developed and modified in a special manner.

§. 43. The Subordinate Character of Rights

Law in the subjective sense is a central point upon the basis of the objective coherence of legal institutions (see above, §. 32 at the end). That is, by virtue of the recognition of personality it is an independent principle which reacts again on the order of the legal institution in which it arises. But the content of the entitlement is everywhere first determined by the nature of the legal institution, and therefore the totality of the legal order can never find its supreme principle and coherence in subjective entitlement. This even holds true for Roman law, where more than in any other legal construction it is an independent principle, in many cases entirely detached from higher considerations.

§. 44. Freedom is Not the Supreme Criterion of a Legal System

According to the subjective-rationalistic conception of the legal system, private law is a *division of rights*, public law a *division of powers*. Here everything is related to the entitled person as center. With the former, the distinguishing category is then the *object* [Gegenstand] *of rights* (rights to things, actions [Handlungen], persons), with the latter the *form of activity of power* (legislative; judicial, i.e., subsuming[76]; executive, superintending power).

This system above all lacks *logical agreement*. Public and private law are erected upon different concepts, and in private law not even the category of object can be implemented. So for example, property and servitudes have the same object, the thing, and are distinguished only by their *content*, i.e., the acts allowable upon the object; the right of pledge through its conditionality, its dependent nature, etc.[77] Furthermore, this system does not answer to the requirements of a *juridical* system, because its principle of distinguishing – law in the subjective sense or even the object according to its variation – is not the

---

[76]Subsumption: "A narrative of the alleged crime, specifying the manner, time, and place of the crime, the person injured, etc." *The Compact Edition of the Oxford English Dictionary* (London: Book Club Associates, 1979) – RCA.

[77]When it is said that with property the object of the right is the thing, while with easement it is the usage, this is unacceptable; one should much rather say: the object with property is complete usage and complete disposition, while with easement it is only particular usage. This is however not an object in the sense that things and actions initially were declared to be objects of rights, but rather *content*. In the same way, the innermost essence of the law of pledge is not expressed when one describes it as the right to the *value* of a thing, it is much rather the dependent nature, the purpose to serve as guarantee for another right, which constitutes its peculiarity, and not the distinction of objects.

principle which *brings about* [bewirkt] juristic determinations. For example, it is certainly not any distinction of objects that by reason of the legatee the third form[78] must be passed up [sich die Quarta absiehen lassen muss], or that children cannot be disinherited; rather, it is the nature of inheritance as a legal institution. Finally, this system only includes a *separation, classification;* it does not indicate, as the term speaks to [wie das Wort anspricht], the interrelation. How thereby "the organic relation of rights to one another and to the whole, the members of which they are"[79] is indicated, simply is not discernible [nicht abzusehen]. This whole is in fact nothing other than the legal order. Starting from the legal order and thus legal institutions, one arrives entirely naturally, in fact of necessity, at rights; but starting from rights one will never arrive at legal institutions; the matter remains a plethora of rights. On the contrary, here the natural coherence is disrupted, so for example one must, to be consistent, classify the right of succession in a different category than the right of inheritance, and legacy [das Legat] must appear in both real rights and personal rights (vindicationis and damnationis).

Disregarding all objections, this system in recent times has found in Puchta an advocate as consistent as he is persistent. It is based on Puchta's *conception of law itself,* as lately has found especially clear expression. For him, the essence of law is not *order* but *freedom,* and the entire content and purpose of law even in the objective sense is *simply the recognition of personality and its will,* its freedom. "The fundamental concept of law is freedom."[80] "Law accordingly is the recognition of legal *freedom,* which expresses itself in the person and his will, and its effect on objects. It is itself a will, firstly God's, and then of the total-

---

[78]i.e., high school education – RCA.

[79]Puchta, *Pandects,* 1ST ed., VI.

[80]Puchta, *Lectures on the Institutes,* 1841, p. 4.

ity of men, who are joined through it, a will *aimed at the recognition of the person and his will.*[81] But is not law, precisely in accordance with this pronouncement, itself much rather order than freedom; for "a will of God" cannot be understood as the freedom and entitlement of God, can it? And with regard to rights does the divine will (or the collective will) truly concern only the recognition of personality and its will and not also the maintenance of certain bonds and rules in human community over men as sacred orders in themselves, which are His will and not the will of human personality? In any case, according to this the question of system shows itself to be a mere corollary and leads back to a quite simple viewpoint: if law is *primarily freedom* and entitlement (so that law in the objective sense is none other than the recognition of this freedom or rights), then, I concede, the system of law is a coherency of *rights*. If however law is *primarily order* (and freedom is only one side, one part of the content of this order), then indisputably the system of law is a coherency of orders, that is, of legal institutions (see above, §. 34).[82]

---

[81] *ibid.*, p. 11, 12.

[82] Puchta's reply to me (*Textbook of the Pandects*, 1ˢᵗ edition, 1838, p. VI) is based on a complete displacement of the point at issue. In no way did I oppose the *factual* (relations) to the *juridical* (legal institutions), as is here conceived, but the *objective* (law and its institutions) to the subjective (entitlement and its objects). I have nowhere otherwise expressed myself than in joining both together: "a coherence of legal relations *and legal institutions,*" and then "complexes of facts *and their legal norms.*" Where I asserted the *factual* (complexes of factual relations), it did not occur in opposition to the juridical but in opposition to the merely *logical*, in opposition to the *abstract category* of object (e.g., in the case of the law of pledge etc.; see above). The conception that the *purpose of life-relations* (which I express alternatively as "τέλος," "inward striving," "drive" of life-relations) is the principle from which juridical statements [Sätze] proceed, and that the ethical power of law draws on the (factual) life-relations [an den (faktischen) Lebensverhältnissen hinzieht] in order to subject them to itself, and therefore likewise that the sequentiality within the system depends upon the factual sequentiality and real reciprocal action of life-relations or legal institutions, as the case may be – this conception certainly is not the *subordination* of the legal to the factual,

is it? It is not otherwise in Puchta's system, so that here as well the ethical, the will of the person, draws on the *factual of objects*, and has this factual as its basis, its Wrst. In this respect as well, Puchta's system makes *factual* relations its foundation, for the variation in object (thing, action, etc.) is undeniably factual. The divergence in our conceptions therefore certainly is not located here. That entire argumentation that it is not the "factual substrate" but the juridical that must be the main issue for a juridical system therefore is not appropriate to the question being dealt with here. Furthermore, it would be well to keep in mind that the system does not have its locus in its results but in its ruling principles. Rights, i.e., that which is owed to you and I, are of course *juridically relevant results*, but the system rests on the principles of the legal institutions by which it comes about that we have such and such rights and according to which it is decided whether we have them, and that is of no less juridical interest.

Puchta has now, despite these decisive objections to the system of *relations*, nevertheless lately expressed himself thusly:

"The personality of man and thus his *legal relations* differ according to how they are conceived in the following characteristics: 1) as individual, 2) as a member of an organic connection: a) the family, b) the people, c) the church. *Legal relations* are distinguished in accordance with this distinction into property, family, public and ecclesiastical legal relations, and the law itself into private law (property and family law), public law, ecclesiastical law" (*Institutes*, p. 54). This cannot possibly mean, as the words seem to indicate, that legal relations follow after the characteristics of men as members of a family or the state. For this would be a reversal of things. Consequently it can obviously mean nothing other than personality and the rights of man are determined in accordance with the legal relations of property, family, state and church. Legal relations are therefore that which primarily determine, the rights of man that which are determined. The system is located however in that which determines and not in that which is determined!

Therefore in the most recent edition of the *Pandects* Puchta has dropped his previous system of obligation according to object and, as in my case (1st edition, p. 152), accepted the foundational division in "obligations of transaction and tort" as well as a broader implementation according to the content of the obligations. Accordingly our controversy regarding system should be ready for conclusion. Whether, however, the cornucopia of damning epithets contained in his preface, awakened by zeal against my entire legal philosophy, was justly poured out on it – at this point in time (1854) I believe with my colleagues and friends that I no longer need to argue about that.

Chapter Eight
Private Law and Public Law

§. 45. The Legal System Reflects the Dual Relation of Common Life

The entire legal system is divided into two main areas. To wit, in accordance with the dual relation of human common life, legal relations are of two sorts. The one serves to satisfy the *individual person*, to complete his existence (of course, only to the degree that it forms an element of the common condition); the other serves to rule men collectively, to join them into a common existence and to complete it as such. The former make up *private law*, the latter *public law*.

Accordingly, the relations of private law are the integrity and freedom of the person, property [Vermögen], family; the relations of public law are state and church.[83] That which is a function or part of the state naturally belongs for this reason to the category of public law – thus municipal law, welfare and criminal law, civil procedure, the law of nations. A relation can however belong to both areas according to its various as-

---

[83]"Publicum jus in sacris, in sacerdotibus, in magistratibus consistit" (I. I. §. 2 *de just. et jure*).

One may view the church since it has been separated from the state by Christianity and especially the Reformation as a third entity alongside private and public law to the degree that it is conditioned by subjective faith and accordingly both the participation of individuals and the recognition of the state is arbitrary and fortuitous. In that case, then, the church appears *relatively*, namely to the people who do not believe it, and the state which does not recognize it, as a mere *private affair*. But in itself and for those who share its faith, it is always and of necessity a *public* institution no less than is the state, i.e., just such an institution which binds them into one subject and rules them by necessity.

pects.[84]

The essence of public law is customarily sought in the *common utility*. But its essence is not the common utility as goal, but the *common rule* (union into one common condition) as object and content of relations. What is public is not simply that which serves the utility of all but that which serves a *higher order* over all utility. The other viewpoint leads to consequences such as public punishment having to target the common utility (protection) – the relative theory – or public power only having as goal the utility of men and therefore put at the disposal of those for whom it is of use, etc.[85]

§. 46. Private Law for Individuals, Public Law for the Community

Man stands in the relations of private law by virtue of his independence and personality and as a whole for himself; in the relations of public law, he stands subjected to a higher power and as part of the human community which in its unity has commandments and goals over itself. The former therefore are realized by individuals, the latter through the act of the community. Hence, in private law the individual is always the goal of the arrangement [Anordnung], even when the manner of arrangement conforms to public goals; in public law, it is the whole. In the former, men always appear as individuals

---

[84]Thus e.g. the relation of ranks, i.e., their delineation, their place in the state (requirements on and privileges of nobility, guild ordinance, freedom of trade and the like) are part of public law, while the modifications which act upon ranks in their other private relations (family trust – inheritance of farmers – commercial and exchange law) fall under private law. Civil procedure (the order of the practice of civil law) is a part of public law, albeit, in terms of the points of issue here treated, with a private-legal side.

[85]The Romans expressed themselves indeterminately: "quod ad statum rei publicae spectat – ad singulorum utilitatem;" even so, this describes the public *condition* more than it does the common *utility*.

— apart or joined with individuals — in the latter, only in the greater community. That concrete private relation therefore is a relation among *specific persons*, that public relation is however one of *objective* institution [Anstalt]; the former therefore ceases to exist with a change of personnel, the latter does not. An obligation, a state of marriage, a guardianship is no longer the same obligation, marriage, guardianship, when it no longer exists among the same persons. Against this, the state is and remains this state through all changes of generations. In the same manner, the civil and criminal procedural law of a state remain the same regardless of changes in individual legal transactions and transgressions.

§. 47. The Effect of Public on Private Law and Vice Versa

Public law encompasses private law to the degree that the latter is conditioned by position (membership) in the commonality and achieves the security of its execution through public institutions [Anstalten] (legal prosecution).[86] Against this, the right and freedom of the person have no less significance for public as for private law. Man is the center for both.

§. 48. The Proper Delineation of the Spheres of Private and Public Law

---

[86]Bacon, *op. cit.*, aphor. 3 and 4. [3. But private right lies under the protection of public laws; for law guards the people, and magistrates guard the laws. But the authority of the magistrate is derived from the majesty of the government, the form of the constitution, and its fundamental laws; whence, if the political constitution be just and right, the laws will be of excellent use; but if otherwise, of little security. 4. Public law is not only the preserver of private right, so as to keep it unviolated and prevent injuries, but extends also to religion, arms, discipline, ornaments, wealth, and all things that regard the good of a state. — RCA.]

In earlier times confusion was brought into the distinction between private and public law, as for example in putting the church and welfare arrangements under private law, the family under public law, primarily on the grounds that one conceived these concepts as a division of *legal norms* (laws). To wit, just as the entire legal system is a system neither of laws nor of authorizations [Befugnisse] but of legal relations and legal institutions, so also this indispensable fundamental division. *Legal norms* in analogous manner may also be divided into public and private, that is, those which are given in the *public interest* and those which are given only for the *advantage of the individual.* The latter can be *altered* by the entitled in his case, the former cannot.[87] But this latter division, although of great practical relevance, nevertheless cannot form the foundation of the legal system. Nor does it in any way coincide with the first. Private law is full of determinations having public interest (are publici juris) and public law often contains determinations to the advantage and at the disposal of the entitled (e.g., civil servants). Should one ask whether the family, welfare administration, the church belong to public or private law, one of necessity intends the division of legal institutions, since family, church are institutions and not norms; upon answering the question, however, one substitutes unawares the division of legal norms, since one has not based the question at all on the concept of relations and institutions, and consequently one reckons the family to public law because many of its determinations exist in the public interest and therefore are immutable, and vice versa. In this manner, one asks with one concept and answers from another. The Romans used the same expression

---

[87]"Jus publicum pactis privatorum mutari non potest," l. 38, de pactis. Just the same is intended where it says "reipublicae interest, dotes salva este" or "testamenti factio non privati sed publici juris est;" for this reason dos and testament in no way form part of public law.

for both divisions, without however mingling the matter. In the first edition of this work I used for the latter division the designation "prohibitive and dispositive norms." More appropriate perhaps is the designation now proposed by Savigny: "absolute and mediating law."[88]

In the same manner one may divide *law in subjective sense* into public and private (§. 35). Private rights are those which have the satisfaction and advantage of the entitled as content and goal, even though in relations of public law; public rights are those which have as content their influence on the whole, and thus as their final goal a consequence for the whole. Accordingly, not simply property, paternal power etc. but also the right of domicile [Indigenat], right of emigration [Auswanderungsbefugniss], tax exemption [Steuerfreiheit], etc. are private rights, while royal warrant [königliche Befugniss], mediatized status of erstwhile imperial nobility [standesherrliche Qualität], estate suffrage [ständisches Wahlrecht], freedom of the press and the like are public rights. Nor does this division coincide in extent with that of public and private law. An application of it will be made when discussing the doctrine of the boundaries of legal procedure [Gränze des Rechtsweges].

---

[88]See my first edition, II. I. p. 125, and Savigny, *System of the Modern Roman Law*, I. p. 58.

Chapter Nine
Civil Justice and Equity

§. 49. The Forms of Civil Justice

Civil justice is only the expression in the area of civil order of the eternal essence of justice as already set forth (I. §. 55). It is ever a determining power for the original construction of law; in particular, it is the power for its maintenance through protection and retribution.

Protective justice is instigated by the *disturbance of another's rights.* This can be either of a negative sort, *nonfulfillment* (e.g., nondelivery of a legal object, nonperformance of an owed service), or of a positive sort, *infraction* (e.g., damage to things, overcharging). The expression of justice in the former case is the command of fulfillment, in the latter compensation, in both cases in the final analysis coercion. With infraction, the act of the disturber is the decisive consideration, with nonfulfillment it is simply the entitlement of the one disturbed, which is why in the former case accountability (dolus, culpa) is presumed while in the latter it is not; meanwhile nonfulfillment, continued with awareness, in fact becomes infraction. However, neither appears as an instigation of retributive justice, as being punishable. Certainly, every knowing and willed disturbance of the rights of another, and especially by infraction, infringes the commandment, and infringement of the commandment, in accordance with ethical principle, is generally an offence to higher regard, which calls for punishment. Nevertheless, because the civil order as mere external order does not challenge the mind of men, it is therefore no infringement of its regard that the subject not voluntarily perform what is owed (be it either the initial fulfillment or the commanded indemnification), instead allowing it to come to coercion.

Against this, *retributive* justice is instigated by the *infringement of the civil order as such.* This is the case when the violation either affects an unrecoverable [unherstellbaren] object of the legal order (e.g., life, state constitution) or a recoverable object in such a manner that the perpetrator precisely aims at evading the redressing public power (theft, criminal deception). For that is *active* frustration and thus destruction of the legal order, not the mere *passive* awaiting of punishment. This is the concept of *crime*, and its consequence in terms of justice is punishment as restoration of the regard for the violated legal order.

Protective justice only issues a command to the disturber (conviction, determination regarding compensation); when he fulfills this, the public power does not intervene (execution), in that all that matters here is satisfaction of the one disturbed. Against this, retributive justice requires that the redress simply be carried out by the public power, since only in that manner does the majesty of the civil order preserve itself over the criminal, punishment is therefore only punishment if carried out by the ruling authority.

§. 50. Equity as Opposed to Justice

Equity forms an opposite to justice. The essence of justice is to maintain a given order, law and right inviolably intact, while the essence of equity is precisely *disregarding* all prior existing order, all prior conferred law and right, simply to restore the *equality of advantages and disadvantages* (aequum) among those concerned. So for example the Law of Moses provides that when one's ox gores another to death, the living and the dead will be common to both. The right of the former, which according to justice must be accorded if he does not forfeit it, is thus left out of consideration. This might be an unconditional quantitative equality or even a proportional one in accordance with the measure of the needs of those involved or their having caused (through no fault of their own) damages, etc. One often however reckons considerations to equity which are grounded in justice and are not considered in positive law only due to its shortcoming. Considerations of this sort are especially contained in the equity system of the Romans (bonum et aequum) which they oppose to their system of strict justice (strictum jus), such as e.g. compensation, defense of fraud.[89]

In terms of its deeper root, equity rests partly on the original equal entitlement of men and partly on the equal love for all, which yields an equal standard everywhere where no special law, right, or right-founding act effects a preference. In this root, equity is reunited with justice, it consisting merely in disregarding those intervening grounds. A decision in accordance with equity is therefore in order where such facts grounding a specific inviolable right are truly lacking, e.g., in the settling of confused boundaries,[90] while in the contrary case it is a censurable violation of justice. Only the entitled himself may forfeit his right and exercise equity. Equity is only to fill in the gaps left where justice does not extend. We therefore do not attribute equity to God, since his justice fills all things.

Legislation may follow the principle of justice or the principle of equity, and thereupon the function of the judiciary can be referred to the one or the other. The principle of justice expresses itself differently with regard to legislation than with regard to the function of the judiciary, in that with the former

---

[89]The Roman exceptio doli, in which a person who is sued may plead fraud on the part of the plaintiff – RCA.

[90]To this category belong e.g. cases in which the Romans were wont to appoint a majority of judges (arbitri, superatores).

it consists in the consistent implementation of law-ideas in each and every institution, with the latter in the consistent implementation of specific (derived from the law-ideas) *statutes* and *positive-legal* principles. The consistent upholding of granted entitlement is the same in both respects. To the degree that the function of the judiciary depends on equity, any objective norm of decision-making expressing the national conviction is lacking, in that the equality of advantages and disadvantages merely attaches to the particularity of the case; the judge therefore is simply referred to his own personal judgement. Hence he is not a actually a judge (judex) but only an *arbiter.*

Works Cited by Stahl

Aquinas, St. Thomas. *On the Government of Rulers* [De regimine Principum: various editions]. Cited on p. 26.

Aristotle. *Ethics* [Presumably the Nichomachean Ethics; various editions]. Cited on p. 35.

Aristotle. *Politics* [various editions]. Cited on p. 56.

Bacon, Sir Francis. *The Advancement of Learning*, edited by Joseph Devey. New York: P.F. Collier and Son, 1901 [1605].Cited on p. 59, 69, 71.

Beseler, Georg. *Popular Law and Learned Law* [Volksrecht und Juristenrecht]. Leipzig: Weidmann, 1843. Cited on pp. 74, 85.

Eberti, *Journal* [Zeitschrift; further information lacking]. Cited on p. 86.

Fichte, J.G. *Contribution to the Rectification of the Public's Verdict Regarding the French Revolution* [Beitrag zur Berichtigung der Urteile des Publikums über die Französische Revolution]. Berlin: 1793. Cited on p. 106.

Fichte, J.G., and F.I. Niethammer. *Philosophical Journal* [Philosophisches Journal einer Gesellschaft teutscher Gelehrten]. Jena; Leipzig: Gabler, 1795-1800. Cited on p. 29.

Hegel, G.W.F. *Philosophy of Law* [Grundlinien der Philosophie des Rechts], 5th expanded edition. Hamburg: Meiner, 1995. Cited on pp. 28, 35.

Homeyer, C.G. *The Saxon Mirror* [Der Sachsenspiegel]. Berlin: Dümmler. 1835-1844. Cited on p. 109.

Justinian, *Corpus Iuris Civilis*. Cited on p. 60, 119, 122.

Kant, Immanuel. *Doctrine of Law* [Rechtslehre; many editions]. Cited on p. 99.

Kirchmann, J.H. *The Uselessness of Jurisprudence as a Science* [Die
Werthlosigkeit der Jurisprudenz als Wissenschaft: ein Vortrag].
Berlin. 1848. Cited on p. 86.

Leue, F.B. *German Lay Tribunals* [Das deutsche Schöffengericht] Leipzig :
Kollmann, 1847. Cited on p. 86.

Maurenbrecher, R. [editor's surmise] *De auctoritate prudentum*. Bonnae:
Weber, 1839. Cited on p. 70.

Melanchthon, Philip. *Philosophiae Moralis* [Moral Philosophy; further details lacking]. Cited on p. 26.

Melanchthon, Philip. *Loci Communes* [various editions]. Cited on p. 35.

Puchta, G.F. *Lectures on the Institutes* [Cursus der Institutionen; presum-
ably vol. I: Introduction to Legal Science and the History of Law
among the Roman People (Einleitung in die Rechtswissenschaft
und Geschichte des Rechts bey dem römischen Volk)]. Leipzig:
Breitkopf und Härtel, 1841. Cited on pp. 101, 115.

Puchta, G.F. *Pandects* [Lehrbuch der Pandekten], 1ˢᵗ edition. Leipzig,
1838. Cited on pp. 115, 116.

Puchta, G.F. *Pandects* [Pandekten], 2ⁿᵈ expanded edition. Leipzig: Barth,
1844. Cited on p. 64.

Puchta, G.F. *Pandects* [Pandekten], 6ᵗʰ expanded edition. Leipzig: Barth,
1852. Cited on p. 101.

Richter, A.L. *Textbook of Ecclesiastical Law* [Lehrbuch des katholischen
und evangelischen Kirchenrechts: mit besonderer Rücksicht auf
deutsche Zustände], 4ᵗʰ edition. Leipzig: Tauchnitz, 1853. Cited on
p. 96.

Savigny, F.C. *System of the Modern Roman Law* [System des heutigen
römischen Rechts], vol. I. Berlin: Veit, 1840. Cited on pp. 109, 123.

Savigny, F.C. *The Vocation of Our Time for Legislation and Legal Science* [Vom
Beruf unserer Zeit für Gesetzgebung und Rechtswissenschaft].
Hildesheim: Olms, 1967 [reprint 1840 ed.]. Cited on pp. 3, 60.

Schelling, F.W.J. *Lectures on the Method of Academic Study* [Vorlesungen über die Methode des academischen Studium]. Tübingen: Cotta, 1803. Cited on p. 28.

Schleiermacher, F.D.E. *Ethics* [Ethik: (1812/13): mit späteren Fassungen der Einleitung, Güterlehre und Pflichtenlehre]. Hamburg: Meiner, 1981. Cited on p. 29

Stahl, F.J. *The Philosophy of Law According to the Historical Perspective: Vol. I: The Genesis of Current Legal Philosophy* [Die Philosophie des Rechts nach geschichtlicher Ansicht: 1. Bd.: Die Genesis der gegenwärtigen Rechtsphilosophie], 2nd ed. Heidelberg: Mohr, 1830. Cited on p. 29, 105.

Stahl, F.J. *The Philosophy of Law: Vol. I: The History of Legal Philosophy* [Die Philosophie des Rechts: Band I: Geschichte der Rechtsphilosophie], 3rd edition. Tübingen: Mohr, 1854. Cited on pp. 28, 99.

Stahl, F.J. *The Philosophy of Law: Vol. II: The Doctrine of Law and State on the Basis of the Christian World-View: Part I: General Doctrines and Private Law* [Die Philosophie des Rechts: Zweiter Band: Rechts- und Staatslehre auf der Grundlage christlicher Weltanschauung: Erste Abteilung, Erstes bis Drittes Buch: die algemeinen Lehren und das Privatrecht], 3rd edition. Tübingen: Mohr, 1854. Cited on p. 29, 98, 107.

Thibaut, A.F.J. *System of Pandect Law* [System des Pandekten-Rechts], 1st edition. Jena: Friedrich Mauke, 1803. Cited on p. 46.

Warnkönig, L.A. *Legal Philosophy as Natural Doctrine of Law* [Rechtsphilosophie als Naturlehre des Rechts]. Freiburg im Bresgau, 1839. Cited on p. 28.

Weber, A.D. [editor's surmise] *Systematic Development of the Doctrine of Natural Obligation and its Historical Effect* [Systematische Entwickelung der Lehre von der natürlichen Verbindlichkeit und deren gerichtlichen Wirkung]. Schwerin, Wismar und Bützow, in der Boednerschen Buchhandlung, 1784. Cited on p. 46.

Index

ard, 39
as independent order, 8
as inheritance, 72
as objective ethos, 11
as rule versus individual
case, 12
binding power of, 35, 36,
39, 50, 53-55, 62
boundaries of, 19
cannot be separated from
God, 25, 26
constitutional, 45
continuity of, 39, 40, 79
continuity of, as ethical
principle, 73
customary, x, 52, 53, 55, 67,
74, 108
depends on the state, 24
detachment from popular
consciousness, 79
development of, 39
entrusted to the people, 9
ethical power of, 12, 116
excludes individual con-
duct, 12, 13
Germanic law, 35, 82, 86
given positive shape by the
people, 34
ideas of Providence in, 18
in the subjective sense, 97,
98
institutions as object, 12
learned, 65, 70
misrepresented by legal philosophy, 25
nationality of, 78
natural, 39, 44-46, 91

natural versus positive, 36,
37, 46, 47
nature as raw material, 19
negative character, 20, 21,
92
not defined by coercion, 12
not the product of public
opinion, 77
of Christendom, 44
of Moses, 64
of nations, 94
of pledge, 111
of reason, 44
only outward shape of life,
11
order of people and na-
tions, 10
organic growth of, 41, 51,
73
popular character, 77, 83,
85-87
popularity of, 78
positive, 2, 3, 24, 33-42,
45-47, 69, 70, 72, 74,
91, 104, 105, 109, 127,
128
positivity of, 33, 36
private, 29, 80, 81, 85, 103,
104, 107, 112, 114, 117,
119-123
product of human commu-
nity, not public opin-
ion, 77
providential ideas in, 18
public, 29, 39, 81, 103, 112,
114, 117, 119, 120
purpose in, 18

Printed in the United Kingdom
by Lightning Source UK Ltd.
118488UK00001B/112-129